THE POWER OF WHY: 25 MUSICIANS COMPOSED A LEGACY

GLORY ST. GERMAIN

GLORYLAND PUBLISHING

COPYRIGHT

Compiled By: Glory St. Germain

Edited By: Wendy H. Jones and Lisa McGrath

Cover Design By: Glory St. Germain

DEDICATION

To my husband Ray, "my Elvis", for writing his rockabilly hit "She's a Square" and inviting me out for pizza, which led to our amazing life together. Thanks for including me in writing 3 songs on your Christmas Album, and for sharing the songwriting experience that will bring joy to others for many years to come.

To our son David and our daughter Sherry, who produced the Ray St. Germain Family Christmas Album, thanks for your dedication and unconditional love of family support.

And to our 5 children Chrystal, Catherine, Ray Jr., David, and Sherry, and grandchildren Jeff and Catie, for sharing your beautiful voices with the world in singing on the Christmas Album and so many other performances with your dad/granddad.

I love you all.

CONTENTS

FROM IMPROVISATION TO INTENT: MY JOURNEY AS A COMPOSER

Adrienne McKinney
United States

"How... how did you even... think of this," my student, giving me a side-eye-to-remember, asked hesitantly as she sight-read the first part of my newest piano composition. Granted, the piece is titled *Macabre Incantation*, so clearly not a sunny, cheerful tune, but it still made me chuckle to hear that question. "I have no idea," I responded, adding, "I just sat down and played it one day. Maybe it was something I ate?" or something like that. We giggled. She resumed playing the eerie, descending bass ostinato.

In the summer after my junior year in college, I often found myself improvising for hours at a time. Sitting at the piano in our house, just a few blocks from the university campus, I would practice my solos and then launch into whatever melodies, harmonies, and rhythms came to me. Sometimes I set up a tape recorder with one of those ninety-minute cassettes and recorded everything I played. Out of hours of tape, there was one musical idea that stuck with me. I jotted it down in a new notebook and played it for a composer friend, saying I had no idea what to do with this, but it felt good to share it and have it well-received. This became relevant later, but at the time, I didn't know why I wrote it, let alone what to do with it.

Composing was not especially easy for me, or at least I wasn't doing it the way I thought I was supposed to. I envied composers who could seemingly transfer notes directly from their minds onto the page. My technique involved playing first, and then writing it down. "Does this count as real composing?" I always questioned myself. I kept improvising. After a while, I began writing more of my ideas in my notebook. Everything was by hand.

In graduate school, I had an opportunity to study composition as an independent study. I wrote two new pieces, both based on melodies that came out of improvisation. One of them premiered at the spring student composer recital. I felt nervous, yet grateful to be included. Was this my Why?

Years passed, and though I was focused on teaching, I kept my manuscript notebook nearby. Sometimes, I would jot down a rhythmic motive or harmonic progression. I composed so infrequently that I used the same notebook from my college years. "Hang onto these ideas," I told myself. Surely, I wrote them for a reason, even if I wasn't sure what it was yet. Flipping through the notebook, I saw that musical idea I had improvised as a student; the one I shared with my composer friend. I sat down and played it again, a series of broken chords in contrary motion. I played it once more and suddenly knew what to do with it. This little idea, from ten years ago, was really an accompaniment pattern. Of course! I set about writing the solo over it and later it became my *Sketch for Horn and Piano*. This gave me another idea. What if I wrote music for my students? I needed music to supplement the materials I was using to teach beginning piano students.

Here was my lightbulb moment. I began composing with

intent. My improvisations, those aimless sessions that felt like they were just for me, would lead me to write new pieces for my own students. Why didn't I think of this sooner? At the same time, I felt like such an impostor, as though I had missed out, and was too late to the game; there was already so much quality music available, why did I think anyone wanted something I wrote? I worked hard to push those thoughts aside and press on.

What kind of music did my students need? They needed short pieces, music written in a specific note-range, simple rhythms, catchy tunes. I wrote to help my students reinforce the skills they were learning, in musical styles that they would find engaging and entertaining. I wanted to combine old techniques and ideas with new sounds and imagery. *Chocolate Cupcake Machine, Apple Crisp, Spinning Web.* Naming the pieces was more difficult than composing. The titles needed to be exactly right, not too childish, not too dry. Today's students seem more sophisticated than I was as a student – or is it just in my imagination?

The best feeling was having other teachers respond positively to my compositions. I set up a website and featured my pieces online. Still second-guessing myself, I continued to write and share my pieces for piano students, usually in online teaching forums. In 2016, Irina Gorin sought a composer to write a beginners' Christmas collection for her *Tales of a Musical Journey* series. I jumped at the opportunity. I quickly wrote ten little arrangements with original teacher accompaniments. It was such a pleasure, and the challenge was just what I needed. I knew I could compose with intent, and that my pieces could serve an educational purpose and be enjoyed.

So, what about *Macabre Incantation?* Some pieces seem to write themselves. I didn't sit down with this idea, I just started playing, and there it was. How did I even think of this? Jotting as much down in my notebook as possible before entering it into my engraving software, I spent hours writing and revising, playing through and changing, reengraving and publishing. I knew my students would love it. Like several other pieces, if you asked me how I wrote it, I couldn't exactly say, but now I can say why I wrote it.

You may have a collection of musical ideas, too. Some of them may be from years ago. Perhaps there's a reason you wrote them, and it's only now that you know why. I encourage you to dust off your composition notebooks, locate your old MusicXML files, and see what treasures you find. Who knows? You may have the beginnings of a new piece ready to be shared. I wish you the best of luck.

Author Bio:

Adrienne McKinney, accomplished musician, composer, and UMTC Elite Educator, owns and operates McKinney Music Studio and Pianolex Music Publications. She provides personalized, engaging music instruction and composes appealing modern music for pianists of all ages.

https://www.pianolex.com

FAIRIES AND MONSTERS

Dominique Levack
United Kingdom

I remember it like it was last week: sitting on his lap, perched over the piano keys watching his brown fingers expertly whizzing up and down playing a boogie-woogie. It was the most thrilling moment of my young life up to that point. I was five years old and in the canteen of my mother's Art College in Plymouth, UK, being looked after by a piano wizard called 'Malt' while Mum was studying. No crèches back in the seventy's; Mum had to make do with her friend's good will, and I hit the jackpot.

When Mum left the college, she bought the piano, and it came to live in my bedroom - my musical shrine. I arranged all my dolls and teddies on it and proudly sat on top of four large cushions on a chair just to reach the keys. It became my world, and I spent every day playing fairies (high notes) and monsters (low notes) making up stories and reflecting them back to myself using the keys. I had no clue about octaves, or scales, or notation, but I got to know the sounds and the way the shiny ivory black and white keys made me feel.

Because I was self-taught, once I started piano lessons around the age of fourteen, I was like a wild pony, almost impossible to tame. My poor tutor. I much preferred to make up songs about teenage life and hang out with my best friend who played the drums. Practicing scales and learning to read music was like trigonometry torture and I was dragged through the Pianoforte grades kicking and screaming.

However, the joy of creating something in the moment, improvising and song writing has only grown, and I still feel it to be the best way to spend time.

My family moved around a lot, and I rarely stayed at the same school for more than a few years. This caused me a lot of anxiety, always being the new girl. However, I used to find music practice rooms and shut myself away at lunchtime, eager not to be seen - to be alone in the playground. If I were having a particularly lonely day, I would look forward to coming home and spending hours into the early evening at the piano just playing my feelings out.

When Mum called me to start helping her get the dinner ready or feed my sister, I would fly into furious rages, as I wasn't quite ready to stop yet.

Now I recognise this to be a form of music therapy, self-soothing and regulating my emotional state. Looking back at this time growing up, that's all I really did. I sought out other musicians anywhere and everywhere and soon found myself in bands, rehearsing covers in smoky practice rooms twice a week, and playing gigs at weekends. Around the age of twenty, a drummer friend took me to a home studio in Sussex and intro-duced me to Eki. She played the bass and was a sound engi-neer. The combination of her skills and mine made it possible for me to record my own songs easily, so I started to write on a regular basis. Working by day in a smart chocolate shop, I would save up my earnings and drive over to Eki's studio on a Friday evening and move in for the weekend. Around this time, I received The PRS John Lennon Songwriting Award, and we went up to London to meet Yoko Ono and George Martin who presented the award.

This led me towards forming my own band and touring, spending time in other countries, and developing a thirst for composition working across different genres.

Years passed in this way, but when I moved with my young family to Spain, I was unable to take my piano, so turned to DJing for an income. I bought a pair of technics turntables, CD J's and a mixer and played Latin house music at festivals and parties. I don't think I was particularly good technically, but I was the only female DJ around at the time.

I retrained in 2014 at Nordoff Robbins London, in music therapy. This changed the course of my career as I recognised the value that music can have across society within healthcare and wellness, and how profoundly it can help those with disabilities, neurological disorders, dementia, autism, and mental health.

In fact, I've never seen a client not react in some positive way to music. There have been many joyous musical moments along the way including performing live on a British TV variety show followed by a man hypnotising a chicken to support an autistic non-verbal young man singing.

My back catalogue spans over twenty years with works being performed within theatre, short films, and TV. I have had songs picked up for synchronisation and produced instrumentals for production houses.

There seems to be no fixed route to becoming a composer; however, it's important to be versatile and open to challenges. It's also vital to have other professional skills because constant work is not realistic in my experience.

Recently, I released my piano chill out album *Improvisations'* on Bandcamp where I have direct contact with my audience. I manage my page, set my prices, and gain 80% of my revenue.

The explosion of Digital Streaming Platforms (DSP's) has exposed a massive disparity between composers/songwriters and the record labels and tech giants. Musicians did not recognise the impact streaming would have on the music industry. They sign up thinking their music will get wider exposure. This indeed is true, but in doing so they give away their streaming royalties and are being exploited to the point that legislation has had to be introduced. Creators get $0.004 per stream. 1M streams generates $4370. Daniel Ek, founder of Spotify is worth $4.4 Billion.

For me, this is as serious as our global warming crisis. Greed has taken over from ethics and could leave us without a clean functioning world and a lack of music. If writers cannot afford to create, will they simply stop? #fixstreaming and #brokenrecord are causes I support – as the younger generation have got used to free music.

Music has been my north star. It has put food on my table and allowed me a life of joy and creativity. In return, I am now committed to raising awareness of the value of music within wellbeing and healthcare and to support change within unethical DSP's. Like my dear friend Danny Bryon said, "It's good to give back."

Author Bio:

Dominique Levack is a composer, award winning songwriter, educator, and music specialist within music therapy. Music as a means of communication, music as medicine.

https://dominiquelevack.com/

3

THE MUSICAL PAST, PRESENT, AND FUTURE

Frances Balodis
Canada

W hat is a Legacy? A legacy is something transmitted or received from an ancestor or predecessor or from the past. What does it mean to leave a legacy? It means putting a stamp on the future and making a contribution to future generations. People want to leave a legacy because they want to feel that their life mattered... you will live your life as if it mattered.

In writing the music program *Music for Young Children* (myc.-com), I have left a legacy.

When did that happen? Our daughter Olivia and our son Mark were the reasons that *Music for Young Children* was created. It was important to me (as a music teacher and mom) that our children would have a strong foundation in music and would have music to enrich their lives. Our son did learn to play the trumpet, the violin (old tyme fiddle like his grandfather Wesley), harmonica, and the piano. Our daughter Olivia did pursue music at university, both in the United States and in Canada. She is an excellent pianist, flutist, and singer. Olivia and her husband David have owned and directed *Music for Young Children* since 2010. So, music 'stuck' with both of our children. Our grandchildren Quinn and Logan are now enjoying music. Quinn plays the piano and has completed Conservatory Grades and Logan is beginning his musical journey in Sunrise (children in MYC begin as young as 3 years of age).

So, that beginning of *Music for Young Children* in 1980 has now grown into the 2nd generation of family. This is a legacy.

Where else has the legacy been left? The hundreds of *Music for Young Children* teachers and their families also have been putting a stamp on the future of music in Canada and around the world. MYC students and teachers correspond with me regularly, telling me of their successes. A former student who is now studying in Switzerland is thrilled to send me live streams of his concerts. A former student sent me a proud note to say she is now Dean of Music at a Canadian University. This all started with their *Music for Young Children* studies and the nurturing of the love of music and the love of learning music.

How has the legacy been left? Through the ambitious endeavor of training music teachers in the use of Early Childhood techniques, learning styles, and unique music methods to teach *Music for Young Children*. The legacy is through sharing the playful, happy process of 'the happy habit of learning music'. It is important to feel the nurturing of energy through music – and to help teachers, parents, and students understand the value of music education at a young age.

To live your life as if it mattered – yes, this musical life matters. So many folks say, "I wish I had studied music. I wish I could play the piano." As creator of *Music for Young Children,* I have helped my teachers (both young and newly retired from another career) to embark on their *Music for Young Children* journey.

Also, as a teacher I have taught scores of students – some very young, some very elderly. Teaching has enriched and energized my life as I know I am making a difference in the lives of others.

Growing the legacy is mysterious in many ways. I don't know all the ways *Music for Young Children* has touched the lives of others. It has grown from one teacher to nine-hundred teachers around the world. There are 481,057 children who have been in MYC since 1980. Many of those students are now applying to be teachers of *Music for Young Children*, and many of those students are now bringing their children and grandchildren to MYC classes. The value of MYC is long lasting which makes for a strong legacy.

Did this legacy happen single-handedly? No, it grew in a family. For thirty years the business manager of MYC was my husband, Gunars. The original artist, Tim, was the father of three children in the program. The next artist was the mother of two children in the program. When typesetting became possible with computers here in North America, the first typesetter was the husband of a MYC teacher. The coordinators are teachers with MYC teaching and business experience. The staff at MYC Head Office have been people connected to MYC through coming to classes with their children or hearing about the positive work environment and wanting to join the team. MYC is now owned and directed by our daughter Olivia and her husband David. MYC is truly a family.

Why a special legacy? *Music for Young Children* has had a Composition Festival for thirty-four years. The Composition Festival includes MYC students from ages three and up. The compositions are amazing, and the legacy this leaves is astounding. To cite two examples – two of my students are now PhD students in Composition in New York. This started with their compositions in *Music for Young Children*. Who would have thought that these little compositions would lead to world-class award-winning compositions?

That is a legacy.

"What you leave behind is not what is engraved in stone monuments, but what is woven into the lives of others." ~ Pericles. When a choir from Southern Ontario came to our northern part of Ontario, I asked them (teenagers) who were MYC graduates. Several responded in the affirmative. Yes, in every choir or orchestra there will be MYC graduates – who are proud and excited to say they are part of the *Music for Young Children* family. MYC is woven into the lives of many; it has enhanced young and old, rich, and poor.

Did this happen on purpose? I wanted to ignite a blaze of music in the hearts of our children, Mark and Olivia. From that original spark, the fire spread to others. When a fire gets started – it spreads and makes a new path for growth. And that is what happened. One could say *Music for Young Children* 'spreads like wild-fire'.

Author Bio:

Frances Mae Balodis MEd., Children® and cofounder of CLU ARCT, LCCN(H), LCNCM(H), RMT, MYCC is founder (in 1980) of *Music for Young Children*™.

https://www.myc.com

4

A COMPOSER'S JOURNEY

Bradley Sowash
United States

My first attempts to play music were in family jam sessions where we'd all trade licks on tarnished instruments leftover from my parents' stints as big band musicians. Our favorite tune was *When the Saints Go Marching In*, which I learned to play on piano, trumpet, and trombone. Back then, making music was nearly all intuitive. I remember noticing that there seemed to be rules involved (music theory), but mostly, I just tried to play whatever sounded right.

Later, I took lessons from a traditional piano teacher. I mostly remember her heavy cardigan sweaters, the mothball smell of her house, and a sternness that scared me a little. She taught me reading and basic technique, but her formality was nothing like our carefree family jams. So, when I reached an age when quitting lessons was allowed, my music education switched to required listening to classical music, playing in rock bands, and learning from my older brothers. One brother, who played in a blues band, showed me how to improvise from the guitar chord symbols rather than read the written notes in pop song folios. The other brother, who had already written and performed neoclassical chamber music even before studying composition at music school, decided to tutor me in college level music theory. That jump-started my interest in composing piano ditties.

One night, we visited a restaurant where a jazz pianist played tune after tune without reading music. Fascinated, I approached the bandstand to ask him how he did it. He simply said, "Learn your chords, kid," and he was right. I now know that harmony is a font of musical creativity. Later, he became my jazz piano teacher. A bit overconfident, I may not have been his best student. Still, he managed to convey the nuts and bolts of jazz harmony, moved my technical skills forward, and reigned in my undisciplined improvising. This led me to land the piano seat in my high school jazz band, which became my tribe.

I loved hanging out in the band room during free periods to trade licks with bandmates. When I became good enough to attend an out-of-state summer jazz camp, I found that playing with more experienced student musicians was inspiring but oh, so humbling. I think that may have been the first time I realized that I was going to have to work hard to stand out. Around that time, I wrote a chamber music suite that featured in our school concert thanks to a supportive band director. Stunned by the ensuing applause, I froze and had to be told to take a bow. I naively began dreaming about joining the echelon of famous American composers like George Gershwin or Aaron Copland.

Despite my underdeveloped music reading skills, I was accepted into The Ohio State University music department as a composition major. My professors again pushed my piano technique forward and added significantly to my music theory knowledge. Since I rely on those skills every day, I thank them for that but at the time, I found the perfectionism of formal training to be tedious. Since I was accustomed to improvising hours-long gigs by heart, polishing one or two classical pieces over an entire term was not a familiar learning pace. Similarly, my composition exercises felt pedantic. I wanted to write musical masterpieces. What I didn't realize at the time was that I was learning the craft of making music, paving the way for the art to come later.

It was in this sophomoric state of mind that I landed a job accompanying classes in the department of dance. When a modern dance teacher calls out "5, 6, 7, 8," there's no time to deliberate. The accompanist must instantly summon a chord progression, style, groove, and melody to fit the character of the exercise. When it goes well, the energy loop between musician and moving dancer becomes self-perpetuating. That was an important time for me. I thrived on the challenges, felt appreciated, and met my wife-to-be. To this day, I credit my ability to quickly improvise or compose to the spontaneous demands of accompanying dance classes.

After graduation, I became very involved in the New York City jazz scene, taking lessons and playing gigs with established musicians who widened my understanding of American music traditions. I also continued to work with dancers which led to commissions from choreographers and dance concert performances. My most intensive musical growth, however, resulted from relocating to Belgium in conjunction with my wife's concert dance work. With no friends and inadequate French, I had plenty of time to practice and compose while she rehearsed. Through my evening work in piano cafes and jazz clubs, I also found the generally high regard Europeans have for creative music making to be highly motivational.

Returning stateside, I continued developing my personal style while playing in all manner of settings from background gigs to solo piano concert performances to jazz worship services which led to recording nine albums of original music and hymn arrangements. To augment my performing income, I taught jazz piano lessons for which I wrote my own resources. These, along with my growing catalog of sacred arrangements, were picked up by established publishers, increasing demand for more. At the same time, I was attracting commissions from the directors of ballet companies, big bands, choirs, string quartets, and even orchestras.

Have I composed a legacy? History can decide. In the meantime, I see myself as a craftsman responding to the musical demands around me. Need a Christmas classic arranged for jazz combo and choir? Done. Want a non-traditional encore for your string quartet? I'm on it. Although the job descriptions - jazz pianist, composer, multi-instrumentalist, recording artist, author, and educator - sound like separate threads, they actually all overlap in a rich musical life, and I'm grateful to be living the dream.

Author Bio:

Bradley Sowash is a jazz pianist, composer, multi-instrumentalist, recording artist, author, and educator best known for his innovative live online group jazz piano classes, widely acclaimed keyboard improvisation books, and nine solo piano albums.

https://bradleysowash.com/

5

THEY'RE PLAYING MY SONG

Rami Bar-Niv
Israel/USA

I composed, and still compose, music because I can't not compose. I wrote books because I felt I had something to tell the world, both professionally and personally. In addition, it gave me the opportunity to dedicate my works to my loved ones, alive and deceased. The dedications included our son Shai who passed away at age fifteen from the flu, my late parents, Aharon and Genia, my late grandfather, my late uncle and two of his sons. In my autobiography *Blood, Sweat, and Tours: Notes from the Diary of a Concert Pianist*, I also had dedications to the grandparents whom I never knew and who died in the Holocaust. In the Hebrew version of my autobiography, I added a dedication to our daughter-in-law, wife of our son Tal and mother of our four grandchildren, Shiri Bar-Niv, who passed away in August 2000 at age 45. My piano-fingering book was dedicated to my mother who was my first piano teacher, Genia Bar-Niv, when she was still alive, at age ninety-four. I also dedicated original compositions and arrangements to my wife,

Andi, to my son Tal, to my friends in New Zealand, and to the students at my piano camps for adults.

As a child, I made various attempts at composition. My father, who was a self-taught composer, copied some of my works into a manuscript book in his magnificent print-like music handwriting. My compositions at that time were nothing to write home about. Later on, I studied with foremost Israeli composers like Paul Ben-Haim, Ödön Pártos, and Alexander Boskovich. For a long time, I kept my composition desires on the back burner and concentrated on my worldwide career as a concert pianist.My composing career started slowly picking up in 1972. At first, it was songs for various Israeli song festivals and television programs. Many well-known Israeli pop and folk singers sang my songs in public shows, on radio, and TV. My songs won prizes in festivals, were recorded on record albums, and published as sheet music. Upon the request of the Or-Tav Music Publication, I wrote three different books of Israeli song arrangements for the young pianist. Only then did I start composing concert music: first for piano solo, and then for other instruments, voice, and ensembles.

Toccata was my first piano piece. It was based on my song *Uri Tzafon* and was published by "Israel Music Institute" in Tel-Aviv. After Begin and Sadat signed the peace treaty, I was invited to perform my *Toccata* in a recital in Cairo. I made history by being the first and only Israeli to give a concert in Egypt. Then came *Prayer and Dance* that was published by Israeli Music Publications in Jerusalem with more compositions following. I was lucky to have a house performer for my piano works – me - and naturally, I started incorporating them into my concert programs.Later, I arranged my *Toccata* and *Prayer and Dance* for string orchestra and made it into a three-movement piece titled *Israeli Suite*. It was premiered by the Concord Chamber Orchestra in Milwaukee, USA, conducted by its music director Jamin Hoffman.

I loved Ragtime music and composed in that style, too. My main two genres of composition were Israeli music and American music. In both styles I was heavily influenced by my classical-music upbringing and education. In my Israeli music, I was primarily influenced by my composition teachers whose style was called the Mediterranean Style. In my American music, I was primarily influenced by Scott Joplin and George Gershwin. That is not to say that other composers didn't influence me as well. My compositions were also influenced by Jewish music and by jazz. However, the most important thing for me in composing any genre of music was structure and form.

I love quotes and mostly quoted my own music in my own pieces. I also quoted segments of Israeli folk songs when they were relevant in my music as I did in my *Rhapsody in Blue and White* that I based on three Hebrew songs. I used the four notes that make the BACH Motif, B-flat, A, C, B, several times in my music, whether intentionally or unintentionally. These notes appear several times in my *Song Cycle for soprano and piano: Longing for my Father*. Later, I wrote the *Song Cycle for soprano and chamber orchestra* and it was also premiered by the Concord Orchestra. I composed *Longing for my Father* to seven poems by a Holocaust survivor.

I was born in 1945, the year WWII ended – the year the Nazi concentration camp and extermination center, Auschwitz, was liberated. I feel like I stemmed from the Holocaust. I needed to compose my song cycle to commemorate the Holocaust, it was my modest contribution to society – my debt to all the saint angels who died in the Holocaust.

The computer and Internet revolution also affected the publication of my compositions. I realized that I could engrave the music myself. I entered it into music-writing software and brought it to the print shop for copying and binding. I started self-publishing, and it proved a great idea; it allowed for ease of publishing, greater control, and maximum profits. Then I discovered Amazon, Sheet Music Plus, and other music-selling sites and that opened new doors and ushered in yet another new era.

In the early 1970s, I started including in my recitals my own piano-solo version of *Rhapsody in Blue*. Due to copyright laws, I was not able to publish the music of my version. I patiently waited 50 years to be able to do that legally and recently, I published my piano-solo version of *Rhapsody in Blue*.

In 2012, I self-published my book *The Art of Piano Fingering: Traditional, Advanced, and Innovative*. It took many years to collect the material and three years to write it and prepare for publication. I did everything by myself: formatting, pagination, photos, score samples, diagrams, and artwork. It was hard, but I conquered it. I contacted over 100 publications trying to interest them in publishing my book, but no one accepted it. I'm very grateful to all the publishers who didn't accept my book. It is very successful, and I don't have to share the success with any publisher. The book was published in five languages and received fantastic reviews, from pianists, piano professors, and piano magazines.

When I receive warm, loving, and praising reviews of my books, I cry. It's a grand feeling to hear my music performed, whether by an orchestra or by a little girl in Carnegie Hall – what an elation.

Author Bio:

Rami Bar-Niv, international pianist, composer, author, teacher. Born: Tel-Aviv, 1945. Graduated: Rubin Academy of Music, NYC's Mannes College of Music. Founded "Rami's Rhapsody Piano Camp". Authored The Art of Piano fingering, Blood, Sweat, and Tours.

http://www.ybarniv.com/rami

6

COMPOSITIONAL LEGACIES

Kamara Hennessey
Canada

W hile we were browsing through a pet shop, I gave into my six-year-old daughter, Marty's unrelenting pleas to purchase a hamster. At home, she named it Skippy Rascal. I allowed her to keep the pet in its cage in her bedroom. Every night this creature ran a marathon on the squeaky wheel. It seemed that sound was like a lullaby to Marty's ears as she slept soundly through it. However, as my bedroom was next to hers, that annoying sound definitely was not music to my ears. For two years, Marty took much joy in the responsibility of looking after this tiny animal. One morning, when she woke up and went to her pet's cage, she found Skippy laying on his side dead. Needless to say, the hamster's death set off a very sad tone for the rest of her day; Marty was inconsolable.

The next day, to help her through her tears and the pain of grief, I suggested that we write a song as a tribute to her beloved pet. At the piano, I picked out the notes of the melody that she 'la, la, la'd / hummed out' and wrote them down on manuscript paper. With a few changes of her mind on some notes, she finally settled on what she liked best. The melody turned out to be eight measures in length, with upbeats for every two-measure phrase. Since her 'happy', melody had playful rhythms to it, Marty agreed to title her piece as *My Skittish Hampster* (her spelling). I added the harmony notes. On playback she was so delighted by our efforts. I was awarded with "Thanks, Mom. I feel better," and a warm hug and kisses on the cheek.

Last year, while I was getting rid of old papers in the desk drawers, I came across a photocopy of the original handwritten music with Marty's signature on it. This composition is now secured in a bi-fold folder and placed amongst other treasured sympathy cards and mementos preserved in the plastic covers of a photo album. The label on the front cover says: Martha-Ann Ena Hennessey (1983-1994) Memory Album. In the 2021 calendar year where the page is flipped over to June, I am reminded if Marty was alive today, she would have turned thirty-eight years old on June 21; she was my summer solstice baby.

Composing that song with Marty in her grief over a pet (like a family member) that she loved so dearly, and her death - three years after Skippy died - were the catalysts that redirected my energy to dabble occasionally in composing, later to explore and develop my skills in other creative activities - art and poetry - as therapeutic outlets. Inspiration to compose is often spurred on through the written verses of a poem that crosses my path, a personal artwork, or by celebratory events.

In fall 1994, I participated in a twelve-week mom's bereavement support group. The third week was structured for sharing what the funeral experience was like for each of us during the ceremony and internment of our deceased child. One of the moms brought in a poem titled *Apache Prayer* by an unknown author/poet. The poem was given to her by a friend, and it was read at her teenage son's funeral. I, along with the other bereaved moms, was tearfully moved by the sentiments expressed by the speaker, the deceased, in the poem. As such, this poem inspired me to set it to music. A year after my daughter's death, I resumed private theory lessons with another music colleague. She encouraged me to enter my composition in the Class: D of ORMTA Provincial Canada Music Week and Music Writing Competition. Although I was not selected as a winner (1st / 2nd / 3rd / honourable mention), I valued the adjudicator's constructive comments and suggestions on my sheet in places where I could improve. In one of our social meetings that followed the wrap-up of our bereaved moms' group, I gave a copy of my music to the grieving mom in memory and honour of her son. This gesture on my part was embraced with much appreciation and heartfelt thanks and gratitude for giving her such a legacy to treasure.

My young piano students continue to motivate me. For my student D.J.'s seventh birthday, I decided to give him the gift of music. Since he was learning musical concepts in his theory and practical sessions, I decided to compose two pieces: One melody titled *D.J. THE DETECTIVE* and the other *Splish, Splash*. To encourage him to sing, I also wrote the lyrics. To make the pieces more appealing, I used my artistic skills to add colourful illustrations to reflect each title.

Another student, Payton who started music lessons with me in summer 2020, celebrated her ninth birthday on December 21. My present to her was a composition I titled *A Birthday Song for Payton*. I also wrote lyrics to the music. Using the PrintMaster app, I created a cover page using appropriate clip arts to create a design. Assembling the pages together, it turned out to look like an 8x11.5 size Hallmark birthday card. Mom was quite surprised that Payton was presented with such a gift at her last lesson before the Christmas break. Payton was thrilled to include her card amongst all other presents that she received from her family and friends on her special day. I know that sheet music card is one that Payton will not outgrow or discard, as it will become part of her treasured collection of musical resources to revisit / review as her music library expands in each progressive year.

In my Poetry Circle class, an assignment that was given one week was to write a poem based on 'What It Was'. My imagination took me to the eighteenth century as a composer patronized by the nobility. It turned out that the poem was based on having written a Minuet like Mozart. I subsequently composed a piece titled *Minuet in A*; an ideal piece, I thought, for me to introduce a student to explore the history of this dance style in its periodic context. Art is another medium that ignites a spark to compose. Displayed on my wall is a pastel portrait I did of my belly dancing teacher in costume. Each time I look at it. I think of how uninhibited I became through this dance to embrace my womanhood. A composition *The Belly Dancer* dedicated to my teacher Denise is currently in the works.

Author Bio:

Kamara Hennessey is an ORMTA/CFMTA Registered Music Teacher, Composer, UMT Certified Teacher and 'Elite" Educator. Kamara teaches piano and theory. For more information on Kamara you can visit https://www.khpianostudio.com facebook.com/khpianolessons

7

IT TOOK ME A LONG TIME TO GET HERE

Pam Turner
United States

I am a late bloomer. I started piano lessons at age twelve, having been inspired by the pianist at church (I absolutely loved listening to the prelude each Sunday.), and after having bugged my parents for lessons for a while. Finally, we got a piano and a teacher, and the magic began. I was in love with piano from the first lesson and that has not waned one bit after all these years. I recently reconnected with my childhood piano teacher who had moved away three years into my lessons leaving me heartbroken. She still owns the Steinway grand that I played the little John Thompson beginner songs on, the sonatinas that I adored, and everything in between. I was able to get a fabulous photo of a portion of the keyboard, which now hangs in my studio and is one of my most precious possessions. I continued lessons later as a young adult, studying privately with two excellent teachers at Shorter College in Rome, GA.

My Dad was my encourager with music. He would frequently ask me to play while he read the newspaper after he came home from work. While I was in high school, he also bought a second piano that I could call my own, an old upright that he completely rebuilt just by reading a how-to book. He even got the player part working, and that old thing played great. At the time, I was playing for two chorus classes at school and children's choir at church, and my siblings were complaining that I was on the piano all the time and they couldn't watch TV, so I guess an extra piano in a different room was the best solution for everyone.

My teen and young adult years were a rough ride though, and I realize now that I was depressed and suffering from low self-esteem. I thought I was 'nobody' and had less value than anyone I knew. As the intensity of this grew, I decided to move out at the age of seventeen and joined some friends in a nearby apartment. I finished school, got a job, and got married shortly after that. In the years that followed, I found myself in a couple of bad marriages and endured both physical and emotional abuse.

I'm not sure how I found my way out of all of that, but one thing is for certain – piano was part of my life every step of the way. My faith and piano are the two constant fixtures in my life, and I believe that they are intertwined, with faith being the foundation for music and everything else that is part of who I am.

To those who are facing similar circumstances, I would say don't lose heart. It's still possible to find your way at any point in life, regardless of the circumstances you're tangled up in. Once you start to see things clearly, you may realize that your creativity didn't die but rather lay dormant. It's still there, or maybe you didn't even realize it was there, and it will surface once you find your way out of the fog and begin to transform into the person you were created to be. My journey has been a long one, but I don't believe any of it was wasted, and I think *all* the emotions and experiences – both positive and difficult – are evident in my music today.

The first hint that I would compose surfaced several decades ago when I 'heard' an entire hymn arrangement in my head. It came out of the blue and wasn't even one of my favorite hymns, so I was quite surprised. It wasn't one that I had even thought about arranging – in fact, I hadn't thought about arranging *any* hymns at that point. I decided to write it down note by note on manuscript paper and played it for the offertory at church. It was very well received. Still, I didn't do any more arranging for many years.

There are two reasons that I officially began composing and arranging. First, I found that I was writing in the same notes over and over again when students brought their hymnals to lessons. The typical hymnal is too difficult for beginning students and none of the supplemental sacred books on the market suited me, which led to the writing of *The Worship Series*, a collection of books ranging from late beginner to early intermediate levels.

The second factor was that it became increasingly hard to find piano solos suitable for preludes and offertories that sounded great but didn't take a ton of work. Pieces that take a month to prepare aren't always practical for busy church pianists; thus, the *Hymns Refreshed series* was born. My congregation and students gave me wonderful feedback, so I wrote more. I also found that it was satisfying to have personally invested time and creativity in something that enhanced the worship experience for my church.

I eventually added some original compositions and began to develop a line of lyrical contemporary pieces inspired by scripture, filling the need for instrumental music in the church without bringing in secular music. This took the form of my *Scripture Meditations* book, which came straight from my heart as I meditated on each verse and wrote the matching music just as I felt it.

Over the years, I have received many heartwarming words of appreciation and encouragement – some of it overwhelms me with how my music has touched people, inspired them, and provided emotional healing. I don't claim any credit for this myself, but I am extremely glad to be a channel through which music can flow and be a blessing to others. I'm beyond grateful for that day in 1968 when I went to Mrs. Chambers' house for my first piano lesson, and I am convinced that creating beautiful piano music that encourages and uplifts others is my lifelong calling and purpose in life.

Author Bio:

Pam Turner is a piano teacher, church pianist, and composer. Sacred music is her passion, and she writes both arrangements and original pieces. She currently resides in Varnell, Georgia with her husband, dog, and three cats.

www.pamturnerpiano.com

8

TO COMPOSE OR DECOMPOSE?

Mark Matthews
Australia

"To compose or decompose?" That is the question.

I live to compose - and for me not to, means perhaps that I may slowly ebb away.

Composition...is it a compulsion? No. Perhaps a calling, and yes, perhaps a compelling force, a need to compose, to create a body of work that moves people and touches their hearts and elevates their souls. That causes them to respond, to flinch, to giggle, to sit on the edge of their seats, to laugh, to cry or to hold their breath.

I compose piano solos arising from life, love, and friendship...its experiences and its relationships. I find that when I'm in situations with friends and family, loved ones or even enjoying nature, I respond to the emotive moment, the caring word, the loving gesture, and the power or gentleness of the natural environment. Music is in these instances, and it draws me into its irresistible charm. Even in difficult times, in those uncomfortable moments, I am stirred to my core to find what music exists that could reflect the depths of the sorrow, pain, or discomfort that is being endured.

I hear the music in people's voices. I feel it in their attitudes. I see it in their intentions. I hear the melody in the wind through the leaves of the casuarina tree, in the power of the ocean, in the majesty of the soaring eagle, in the contour of a mountain range, and the energy and vitality of people being together sharing life's experiences, both good and bad.

Sometimes, I feel a coercion, a directive, an impulse, to go to the piano keyboard and discover what it is that is in my heart and mind that could possibly mirror the scenario I had just experienced. It's a sense. It's a feeling. It's a whisper from the ether, from the atmosphere, from the realm of the celestial, to capture the moment in music. To not to, means it may never come to life, not be heard by the human ear, perhaps never experienced...ever.

It comes like a rushing wind, and if it is not apprehended, moves on.

It comes like a delicate breeze, barely hinting at what may lie beneath.

It is sometimes sitting there waiting on the keys, perhaps a suggestion of where to start, only then to lead you on a journey...prospecting for gold.

Why do I compose?

To take captive a melody that is waiting to be taken, a

contour that is pausing for a moment near my ear, patient and willing to be welcomed into my mind, so it can be translated from the mystical into the tangible and then onto the tactile stave and come to life from its ethereal and surreal existence, into the world of the human hearing and experience.

I have felt the effect on myself as I discover a melody, an underlying harmony, and a texture that makes the theme its 'unique self'.

I feel the therapy it gives me as I caress the keys and find the magic of the moment in hearing the sound for the first time... the ahh, as it touches my aural senses and triggers my cerebral neurons. The emotion or exhilaration that sweeps over me as I engulf myself in the composition as it emerges from the ebony and ivory. And then of course the urgency to scribe it, to record it, to create a sketch that finally becomes the audial painting, or sculpture that will then be shared with others.

Why did I initially compose? Because I could not resist it. To not do so, would have been a regret, a missed opportunity, a moment lost.

Why did I continue to compose? Because I saw the effect my first piano solo composition had on the audience, as I tentatively offered my initial piece to that student who heard my work for the first time and then felt the euphoria when she wanted to learn it herself. She was enthralled by it. She was drawn to it. She encouraged me with her kind, accepting words of validation.

"It was ok?" Yes. It touched her heart too. Wow, it does impact others as it impacted me.

I was spurred on.

This particular student breathed-in my first half dozen compositions. She inhaled and devoured them. She wanted more and more. I was so encouraged by this that I felt I should continue to hear what I had heard through my 'life moments', take them by the hand and lead them to the 88 keys that eagerly wanted to hear for themselves what the composition could entail.

The half dozen scores became a dozen and *Music for the Heart and Soul, Opus 1* was born. From there, composing has developed into a craft. As a metalworker or carpenter takes a raw element to create some art, I take a thought, a feeling, a reaction, a passion and translate it into a musical artform.

Watching my students perform the compositions and now seeing students from other teachers around the world do the same, makes me realize that a legacy is indeed being left for the generation following. As others are inspired to also learn to listen with the inner ear, to hopefully hear the music that is waiting for them to be uncovered and discovered, almost as if it has already been composed in the realm of the unseen, lying in wait for us, for us to be sensitive enough to find it, to feel it, to embrace it, to write it down, to share it with the world.

Why compose? Because it is life, it is breath, it is the living legacy of a language that indeed speaks, when words fail to do so.

Author Bio:

Mark Matthews is from Wollongong, NSW, Australia. He holds an honors degree in Civil Engineering and an Associate Diploma in Music. He was also National Champion in the Yamaha Keyboard Festival at age eighteen and represented Australia in Japan. Mark is the Composer of over 20 albums of piano solos.

https://www.remarkablemusic.net

9

MUSICAL RIPPLES

Caroline Quinn
United States

I turned sixty this year. Wow. Half of my life is over. What gifts will I leave for others? My musical legacy is my piano students. Teaching with passion, I hope every student experiences the joy of music, inspiring them to share their gifts, and thus making our world a better place.

I can't imagine where I would be without music. Because of music, I blossomed from an insecure girl into a confident musician and empathetic piano teacher. Every success story has its share of twists and turns. My main obstacles were life situations. For years, mental illness tore our family apart. As the oldest child, I felt the weight of trying to support those who were struggling the most. I failed, miserably. Thankfully, my story changed. Living on my own, I discovered a kinder world creating beauty out of ashes. Music, my anchor and ever faithful friend, opened many doors at home and internationally. When I play, I experience a deep satisfaction and renewal. I am particularly inspired when composing and arranging.

Years ago, I was a music therapist at a medical center in Toronto, Canada. Using music as a therapeutic tool in a clinical setting, I was part of a medical team involved in setting goals in a rehabilitation program. Although I was constantly creating short tunes for my sessions, I stumbled into a more serious world of composing when tragedy struck. One of the children in my group died of a brain tumor. Her passing hit me very hard. Even now, when I close my eyes, I can still see her angelic face sprinkled with freckles. I also remember the scar that spread across her bald little head due to a recent surgery. As I started to process my grief, I remember sitting at my piano aimlessly improvising on major seventh chords. It was comforting and cathartic to hear sounds that matched my mood. Playing the chord tones ascending and descending sounded like questions, unresolved questions with no answers. Through this haunting melodic pattern, I was able to begin to express my profound sadness. My first composition was called *Living Without Answers*. Years later, when I played my song again, the healing melody and lyrics once again breathed hope into shattered dreams.

My songwriting program was successful, and I had some breakthroughs working with teenagers suffering from severe head injuries. Individual sessions provided an appropriate place for patients to ventilate expressing their anger and loss. I will never forget working with a young man I will call David. Hit by a drunk driver, this handsome tennis player suffered a frontal lobe injury leaving him completely paralyzed from the neck down unable to complete the simplest task. Our sessions eventually motivated David to express his feelings. Even in his brokenness and utter despair, when we set his thoughts to music, it seemed to bring a little clarity, and perhaps even, comfort.

Due to Covid border restrictions, I was not at my precious mother's side as she lost her battle with pancreatic cancer. I honored my mother by composing arrangements of her favorite hymns. Across the miles, with my phone propped up so we could see her beautiful face, my husband and I sang and played our hearts out. As tears streamed down our faces, we were comforted seeing her mouthing the words as she slipped away to her final home. A recording sent to her loved ones was shared again when her sister passed shortly afterwards. Her music lives on.

On a lighter note, while waiting patiently for my absent-minded astrophysicist professor to propose (LOL), I wrote my first love song. To this day, whenever I play the first few notes of the lilting melody *My Quiet, Gentle Man*, he smiles and gets a little misty-eyed.

Sharing my compositions with others is my gift. Many were pleasantly surprised when I sang my song *Our Song of Praise* at our wedding. Composing requires time for reflection. Songs composed for my students are tailor-made to fit their particular tastes and needs. Anyone can learn to compose individually and collaboratively. When my student's mother died, we wrote and sang *Diana, A Life of Love* at her service. Whether it be a simple tune for my students, or a song composed for a celebration, every word and note is mine.

Given simple chord progressions, students enjoy creating patterns, weaving their own ideas together, and learning to enhance the pieces they are learning with their own ideas. Improvisations can be added at the beginning and end of their songs acting like bookends holding their music together. The freedom to create feeds their soul and inspires them to learn more. Although none of my students are famous composers yet (never say never), an opportunity to compose is worth its weight in gold, transforming the ordinary into the extraordinary.

While teaching a young man struggling with the physical and mental challenges of having Down Syndrome, I was astounded by the impact music played in his life. After years of lessons, this highly motivated student could perform pop tunes, dazzling his friends and family. Miraculously, he was able to perform at his graduation Baccalaureate service. My arrangement, written to highlight his strengths, was a medley of the beloved hymn *Amazing Grace* and *Hallelujah* by the late, great Leonard Cohen. Watching him perform, giving it all he had, was mesmerizing. Playing broken chords expressively and steadily with his left hand as the glorious melodies rang out with his right, this amazing musician lifted all to a higher place.

Songwriting and composing provides a pathway for emotional expression changing moods and perspectives. We can all relate to songs about hopes and heartaches. Do you remember the groundbreaking anthem *We Are the World*? Encouraging millions to reach out to those in need, its message of hope echoed around the world.

As dedicated teachers, we create a ripple effect that spreads far beyond our lessons, inspiring and changing lives. We may never know the extent of our musical legacies. Who knows? Maybe one of our students will be the next Elton John. The possibilities are endless.

Have you introduced your students to the world of composing? If not, now is the time to start. Believe in the process, and let the magic begin. Like ripples on the water, our music will spread through generations continuing to touch many lives.

Author Bio:

Caroline Joy Quinn, ARCT, Bach. Sacred Music, Accredited Music Therapist, Children's author, Piano Teacher & UMTC Elite Educator. She is a Composer, Arranger, Course Creator and Publisher.

https://www.linkedin.com/in/caroline-quinn-78575a42/

10

AHA MOMENTS

Linda Gould
Canada

C an someone consciously compose a legacy? For me, it started with helping one person, and little by little turned into something bigger than life. A legacy is a result, rather than a goal. This book is about the Power of Why, and this chapter explores why I was motivated to spend thousands of hours at a computer writing method books and eventually turning them into online courses for teachers.

It started with Bill Evans - not the famous jazz pianist - this Bill was a customer who walked into our piano store about thirty years ago. He said he wanted to learn to play the piano. Bill was newly retired and there was something he'd always wanted to be able to do - play the songs he loved on the piano. There was a caveat - he only wanted to learn songs he listened to on the radio when he was a teen.

We never know where our legacy will begin. When Bill asked me to teach him non-classical piano, he became my first Why and it became the start of a 30-year journey that continues to this day. Bill became my first piano chording student. My classical teaching career started at age fourteen and I was in my thirties when he walked into our store. I was, as Bradley Sowash likes to say, "A recovering classical pianist," although I prefer to say an enhanced classical pianist. I had wondered why there was a gap in my classical training and was filling it by learning to play with chords and lead sheets (single staff melody with chord symbols).

Teaching a lead sheet is a fast way to play a song, and this was a terrific opportunity to teach my new passion. Our Why is often linked to passion. It is hard for a classically trained pianist to learn to play with lead sheets - it's a different thought process. The bonus of working with Bill, which eventually evolved into adult group piano classes, was that it fast tracked me to becoming comfortable improvising and creating with lead sheets.

I was surprised when the students in my group classes suggested I take all the worksheets and pieces I had composed or arranged and create a course. I had more groups than I could teach (They kept telling their friends, who told their friends.). I asked, "Why?" They responded, if I put it into a course, their friends across the country could take it to their piano teacher and learn to play chords too. Great idea. So many people want to learn to play piano this way. Little did I know how much was involved in creating a course.

Realizing there was a need became the next step. Learning that I wasn't the only piano teacher who struggled with teaching lead sheets and chords, boosted Why to a higher level. When you see a need, and you have the resources to fill it, it creates an energy inside of you that is explosive.

Where did my passion for piano start? I'm three years old and have taken my first piano lesson. Three! Now don't get me wrong, being three and joining one of the many group piano lessons that currently exist for children is wonderful. That wasn't what I experienced. These were private lessons, and the reason was not any 'Mozartian' talent I exhibited. It was my father's legacy or rather lack of. My grandfather, who died before I was born, loved piano, particularly Chopin. Dad refused to learn to play the piano as a child, and his guilt was about to be reconciled by his daughter (me) learning to play. It was a tough start to a long but fulfilling journey.

I think I inherited some of my grandfather's talent. I really loved the piano. Playing Walter Carroll's *Sea Idylls* with crashing waves was thrilling, and our piano tuner discovered I had perfect pitch when I was six years old. The tough part was my dad's 'participation' in my musical training. I am grateful that my parents gave me the opportunity to learn to play piano, but because of Dad's anger, practicing was not a safe, happy time.

There were wonderful experiences. Playing a Bach piano concerto with the Mount Royal College orchestra in Calgary, Canada was one. I was eleven and the conductor was... J.S. Bach. Yes, that was his name. He made the composer of my concerto so real I could almost touch him. The 20th century Bach would pull, what looked like a toilet paper roll, out of a breast pocket and show us his lineage back to great, great etc. etc. Uncle Johann Sebastian Bach.

All our experiences in life, both good and not-so-good, contribute to our legacy. Yours will be unique to you which is why I hope you consider your legacy.

Another joyful memory was accompanying dance classes in my teens. This experience contributed greatly to my sight-reading skills and my confidence. One day, a choreographer from Los Angeles came to Calgary looking for dancers for a project. I was the accompanist, and he asked if I knew how to play *Tea for Two* by ear. I loved transcribing parts of Dad's old records -*Tea for Two* was in my ear - so I gave it a shot. I had never been asked to do anything like that before. It was so much fun. After the session, the choreographer invited me to come to LA to be a rehearsal pianist. I was too young, but my confidence soared.

The journey to legacy is full of unknown twists and turns, and that's the adventure. It starts with one small step and becomes larger than life. Bill Evans learned to play his favorite songs and told me it enhanced his retirement years. I can say I taught Bill Evans to play the piano. I have also had the joy of sharing 'aha' moments with many teachers as they discover they too can think like a chord player.

What if I turned Bill Evans away because I had never taught the way he wanted me to? What would have happened to my Why? What opportunities to discover your Why are present to you every day? Let the adventure continue.

Author Bio:

Linda Gould B.Mus, RMT, ARCT is the author of the *Play Piano Chords Today* method - adding the freedom of chords to classical teaching. Through online classes, she works with teachers who wish to add creativity to their studios.

https://www.playpianochordstoday.com/teachers-corner

11

THREE AND A HALF MINUTES AT A TIME

Benny Ng
Australia

E very time I try
    To get back on my feet
Gravity denies me
Everything I know

Every time I try
    To get back on my feet
Gravity reminds me
That I'm all alone

That is the chorus of my debut single *All Alone*. I have felt that way at many different stages of my life. One circumstance was when I moved to Australia to undertake music studies. Arriving at Sydney in 2007, I found myself surrounded by new people, culture, and places that I had only seen in movies and TV shows.

Excited, yet confused, hopeful, yet overwhelmed, I was drowning in the cacophony of fresh stimuli. I felt isolated and alone because that was the first time I had been away from my family for so long.

However, I knew I had to take on this challenge if I wanted to become a professional musician. I was born and raised in Malaysia. Back then, music was not a part of the school curriculum in my home country. If you wanted to learn music theory or to play an instrument, private lessons were the only way to go. Music was not offered as a subject in universities either.

So, I made a decision that changed my life: emigrating to Australia to obtain a Bachelor of Music degree. The learning curve was steep as I had no formal training in music. Having to cope with life challenges and catching up academically plunged me into a bottomless well uncertainty. Thankfully, I was pursuing my passion and that gave me the drive to overcome adversity.

I have always loved creating things. My childhood was filled with days of building robots with Lego blocks. Being a detail-oriented person, I am drawn to science and technology because I love the structure that is inherent in those fields. Emotions do run rampant inside this heart of mine. Although I manage them well, my emotions are always bubbling just under the surface. It took a bit of soul searching to finally find the perfect vehicle to channel my creative energies, attention to detail, love of structure, and fiery emotions.

Going through rough patches in life gave me all the raw material I needed to create new music. And it poured out of me. I set up a small recording studio in my apartment and started writing and recording songs. Lyrics and melodies streamed through my mind faster than I could capture them. I wrote pages and pages of lyrics and recorded countless melodies to go with the lyrics. Unlike many songwriters, I meticulously transcribed every note of the songs I wrote. I made sure the notes were in the right place and at the right pitch, so they expressed the message of the songs well.

I must have written close to twenty songs and instrumentals during my first years in Australia. One day, I uploaded a song called *All Alone* to a music streaming website called SoundCloud. I did not expect anything more than a few plays, so imagine my surprise when a Sydney music producer reached out and proposed to fully produce the song. He guided me through the whole process and was encouraging and supportive of my music. We eventually worked together for a total of four songs for my debut EP, which was released in 2019.

Shadowary was born and a new fanbase was created. Armed with those recording studio experiences and new insights into music production, I continued to hone my craft as a songwriter. In music, lyric is the element that stands out the most to me. For me to like a song, the lyrics need to be well-crafted because that helps me to resonate with the song's message.

Lyrics and melodies came easily to me; however, chords and harmony remained a mystery to me. I started taking guitar and composition lessons. I devoured books on harmony writing. Slowly but surely, the fog started to lift as I understood more about harmony and chord theory.

Collaborating with other musicians on songwriting was a rather irrational fear of mine. There are so many unknown factors when co-writing with someone you barely know. However, the lockdown period sparked by the COVID-19 pandemic in 2020, finally saw me taking the plunge. Using Zoom web conferencing software, I co-wrote three songs with musicians from different parts of the country. They were rewarding experiences that certainly added to my skills as a songwriter.

Writing songs is the easy part. For many songwriters, when a song is written, it is usually only 60-70% done. The difficult part comes when it is time to rewrite parts of the song and craft them until all elements of the song work seamlessly together as a whole.

For me, I enjoy both processes equally. The writing process is an exciting flow of ideas that needs to be captured. The rewriting process is when ideas are either kept, discarded, and/or replaced - not unlike a typical brainstorming session in a corporate meeting room.

Why do I feel songwriting is my calling in life?

I had a wonderful childhood but a less than stellar high school experience. I was bullied. I felt isolated and alone. I was from a middle-class family while my classmates were from financially rich backgrounds. Always wanting to belong, to be part of a group or a team, I would feel frustrated and depressed when not being accepted by my peers.

Linkin Park's music helped me get through the pain and the loneliness I felt. I realized then that I wanted to do the same for others. Receiving messages from fans saying that I helped them feel less alone by listening to my music was always a delight. It was a sign that I was on the right path.

It is always a special moment when you hear a song that 'gets' you. An instant connection is made because the song speaks to the depths of your soul and what you're going through or have gone through in life.

I want to be a vessel that ignites that spark. I want to write songs that speak to you and help you feel less alone when things are not going right. With my voice as a loudspeaker and my heart as a source, I want you to feel that everything will be alright one day. Three and a half minutes at a time.

Author Bio:

Benny Ng is a rock vocalist/songwriter of *Shadowary*. His music will inspire you and make you feel better when life gets rough. Get free unreleased music and digital merch on Benny's website.

https://www.shadowary.com

12

THE MADNESS AND MAGIC OF DREAMS

Elizabeth Garland
United States

W hen I was sixteen years old, I was on the path to becoming a concert pianist. I won the state piano competition for the State of New Mexico; I practiced four hours a day. By the time I was seventeen, my family life had fallen apart, my childhood home was foreclosed on, and all that remained of that dream was a small spark that barely flickered. I couldn't even look at a piano. It hurt too much. But through an odd turn of events, music found me again. And saved me. And the creativity, passion, and beauty it led to have surpassed all my hopes and dreams.

At twenty-one, adrift and untethered, I moved to Seattle, after studying theatre and psychology at the University of New Mexico. I was working in a café when the universe stretched out its hand in the form of *Twinkle Twinkle Little Star*. The warbly notes came from a piano in the restaurant at the back. I felt a familiar pain, then a twinge of curiosity. The next morning, I tiptoed past the empty kitchen and sat in the dark restaurant at the old spinet. Tentatively, I stretched my fingers toward the keys and felt an impossible sensation- LOVE- as the Adagio from Beethoven's *Pathetique* released me. Polonaises tumbled from out of nowhere. A two-part invention sprang from my giddy hands.

I followed my heart. Fiercely determined, I began studying music again. I was not old. But I was no longer young. And in the arts, it is our tradition to believe only youth is gifted with genius - for women perhaps even more so. I had a hard battle to prove that I could hit the mark. And then, two things happened in a rather quick succession, my grandmother died - leaving me a Steinway and the legal guardianship of my schizophrenic uncle - and I failed a piano jury and became a composer.

My Uncle Augustus 'Gus' was in his seventies, 6'5", sometimes gentle, many times troubled, frantic, morose, or hysterical. Though we had sat across the holiday table from each other many times, I had, honestly, mostly avoided him, unless he was at the piano. He was a remarkable pianist.

"A true genius," everyone in the family whispered, shaking their heads. "IQ of 165. What a shame."

When I became his guardian, he was living in a frigid room in a Catholic retirement home, for my grandmother could no longer take care of him in her late 90s. He was wearing a dirty, threadbare overcoat, hanging loosely on his thin frame. He smoked incessantly on a bench in the dark winter morning. I couldn't bear it.

I found a new home for him, with expert caregivers for a few residents with intense special needs. I provided new clothes, plenty of cigarettes (for better or worse), a comfortable chair, and a piano for his room. I think he felt cared for again. In time, we forged an unlikely relationship, mostly through our music. At times, he would play Chopin, Joplin, and his compositions. I played whatever I was working on or just messed around with melodies. This is how we communicated. The way we connected.

That fall, I was studying a piece by Scriabin and was given strict instructions not to listen to a recording of the piece. Try as I might, I couldn't convince my exacting teacher to relent and play it for me. This was part of the weeding of those who should be encouraged to continue with music from those who must not. No matter how I practiced, I simply could not hear how it should flow.

The morning of my end-of-semester piano jury, I received a call that my uncle had punched one of the other elderly residents and was being removed. I walked on stage, mind whirling. In the audience were the four people I must impress to continue to study in the program. The keys shrunk under my fingers. I bungled the Scriabin. Some passages flew out too fast, others tripped over themselves clumsily. It was an epic fail.

My teacher, a Steinway Concert Artist, met me, noting the sweat stains on my blue silk shirt. "I'm sorry..." I began. Words failed me.

"Yes, yes," she intoned in her clipped way, "Come. I tell you a story."

I nodded, dejected, hoping for words of encouragement to soothe my frazzled spirit.

"Once, there was a violinist. In his youth, very talented. One evening, an important concert. He took the stage. Suddenly, he shakes. His fingers, not his. The music screeching from his bow. Stooping, he walked behind the curtain. A young boy was preparing. The violinist adjusted the boy's bow hold. He corrected his posture. Suddenly, he knew. You see? He found his purpose."

I felt sick. I wanted to run. "I am not meant to be a piano teacher." I wanted to scream. Now, I know many teachers who are amazing humans. I, myself, had been teaching piano off and on since I was fifteen. It is a special profession that forges unique relationships. But it was not my calling.

That evening, I wrote my first composition: a birthday gift for my then-boyfriend-now-husband. It was as if the universe had just handed me a life preserver. I still love that little fledging piece. I began to incorporate elements of wishes, travels, dreams, pain, impromptus, important moments, laments, and adagios.

And the magic began. More divine intervention. I was playing poker with some friends from Santa Fe. "We just finished making our first film," they said. "We just need some music."

I gambled. "I'll do it. I am a composer." And in saying it, I knew it was true.

From that moment, I've sought to follow my instincts and keep the faith while persisting on this road less traveled. I've arrived at incredible places with music. I won the 2019 International Guild Composition Competition, am the 2021 New Mexico commissioned composer, have performed my works at the World Composers Concert in Vienna, collaborated with artists and choreographers, scored a feature-length film, and many shorts and documentaries. God has given me two amazing daughters to inspire me to keep on. I've taught my students to compose, encouraging them never to give up on the power of dreams.

And now, here I sit. The sun is setting on the ocean in the Pacific Palisades near Malibu, and I am soaking it in. All the beauty and the magic of this place and this moment in my life. In a few minutes, I will meet my producer in his studio. And I am filled with gratitude.

Author Bio:

Elizabeth Garland is an award-winning composer for film and documentary. She is the 2019 International Music Guild Composition Winner and 2021 New Mexico Commissioned Composer. Her works have been performed in the US and internationally.

http://elizabethgarlandcomposer.com/

13

MUSIC HEALED ME

Connor Derraugh
Canada

I was five when I started music lessons, and it was love at first note. I studied classical piano and music theory with Glory St. Germain and found my passion. What a blessing, as music would go on to save my life.

When I was twelve, I attended my first University of Manitoba Summer Jazz Camp. I was shy, green and tentative, the youngest in the program. But by the end of the week, I was sold: 'this is what I want to do, go to the U of M and study jazz.'

Later that year, jazz piano legend Oscar Peterson passed, and I was saddened. One of my early heroes, I was inspired to write a piano piece in his honour. Months later, I performed my composition at Oscar's tribute concert, recorded by CBC national radio. As I stood to acknowledge the rousing standing ovation, I realized that my music had connected with the crowd. Chills swept my body, and I knew then that I wanted to be a professional musician.

In May 2010, however, at fifteen, my journey took a major

detour. During surgery to repair a badly deviated septum in my nose, there was a severe complication. I suffered a traumatic brain hemorrhage, plunged into a coma, and was paralyzed on my right side.

Aptly enough, my first conscious words were sung not spoken. With the Beatles *Blackbird* playing in my hospital room, I woke to sing along briefly - shocking my brothers who were visiting - before slipping back into la-la land.

While re-learning how to walk in the hospital, my right arm limp, my right leg dragging like Quasimodo, I looked up at my dad who held me by a support belt and announced, "I'm going to Jazz camp this summer and there's nothing you can do to stop me."

My dad was highly skeptical but didn't let on saying, "We'll see."

After a month in the hospital, I returned home, spotted my old pal the piano, and sat down to play. Try as I might though, I couldn't make a sound with my right hand. I was devastated.

But fast forward to August and there I was at jazz camp, stubbornly playing the keys with my left hand only. I was in rough shape, but I was determined - my love for music drove me.

Grade 10 began soon after this at an out of district high school that I'd chosen for its renowned music program before my injury. I was scared and lost– at a new school with no friends trying to cope with a new disability.

Fortunately, the school's music room became my refuge. Incredibly, my jazz teacher Bill Kristjanson had such faith that he advanced me to Grade 12 Jazz Band - where I played for all three years. Despite my age and deficits, it was where he felt I belonged.

The band's drummer Cole Ediger recognized me from jazz camp and welcomed me. Cole took me under his wing and became my friend when I needed one the most.

Meanwhile, jazz saxophone great Walle Larsson heard my story and believing that sax would be easier for me to play than the piano, taught me a technique that relied more on reflexes than finger strength. Before long, I was playing music with two hands again.

My challenges went beyond the physical, however, as my brain injury caused a condition called Executive Dysfunction, causing academic difficulties. But with the support of my parents, teachers, and tutors, I managed to get my high school credits and was accepted into the U of M jazz program on saxophone in 2013.

Though sax was now my primary instrument, I continued to doggedly work on my right hand's dexterity, spending an hour on the piano each day improvising to rhythm tracks with my right hand, while playing brain games on my iPad with my left. I know it sounds split-the-brain crazy, but it worked. In fact, I still do it every day.

My tenacity paid off as the piano became my double major.

In the process, I unwittingly developed a unique left hand dominant technique. Being that I write on the piano, my distinctive style is also reflected in how I compose.

My degree took me six years to complete as I continued to struggle with the academic requirements. But like high school, many wonderful people helped level the playing field for me. I found a way to succeed, fulfilling my long-held goals, graduating to become a professional musician.

I've faced many roadblocks - a journey that I share at schools in my multi-media presentation, 'Music Healed Me.' Although I set out to inspire the students, ironically, it's often the students that inspire me when they share their stories. My message is: we all face challenges in life, but with a positive attitude and the power of music, we can overcome any obstacles in our way.

I've learned that to write music, it can't be forced; it must come naturally. Pre-injury, composition came easy. Post-injury, I found it arduous and sporadic. I don't know if it was all the energy that it took for me to heal and get through school, or if it was just the natural progression of my recovery, but composition was the last piece of the puzzle to return.

Unfortunately, it took tragedy to trigger it. One morning we got a call from Cole Ediger's dad telling us that Cole had passed in his sleep. My world was rocked; my best friend was gone.

That afternoon, I approached the piano and a song poured out of me, a complete piece – beginning to end, all in one take. It was the first time I'd written a song like this, based solely on emotion. The tears flowed and the music came. Since then, many more songs have come. Heartbreak unlocked the music inside me.

I'm currently working on a CD dedicated to Cole. Crafting this project has helped me channel my grief into something positive that I hope people will be touched by. It's an exciting time as I can't wait to share my music with the world.

Without music I'd be about a quarter of the way back to where I am. Music has given my life purpose, happiness, and community - a place to turn to when the going gets tough and an outlet to express my ideas and feelings. For me, music has truly been the best possible therapy.

Author Bio:

Connor Derraugh is a Canadian music educator, composer, and musician. A University of Manitoba Jazz Studies graduate on sax and piano, Connor has performed at the Winnipeg Jazz Festival, Mardi Jazz and the Assiniboine Park Concert Series.

www.cdmusic.ca

14

THE WISHING WELL

Eric Carlson
United States

"Her daddy left; his love was spent. She heard the door close again. But a muffled cry from mama's room told her that daddy won't be home soon. The wishing well will be tapped again tonight... oh mama and daddy, can you make it right?"

Those words are the first verse to a song called *Wishing Well*, written by Laurie and Phil Adams, and inspired by a true story. Laurie is my older sister, and when she and her husband Phil first sang this song to me thirty years ago, I bawled my eyes out. Our parents are divorced, and this heartfelt song really hit home. My emotions just came pouring out, and Laurie and Phil knew the song would have that same effect on many others as well. It was their hope that by stirring the listener's heart, perhaps there would be fewer broken families.

I was being tasked with creating a symphonic arrangement so we could record this and other songs for their upcoming album. Music was a refuge for us – a way to dive deep into our souls, to comfort us in our pain and to try to make sense of the insanity – while also helping others. Music has the power to heal and to bring comfort, and it has always served that higher purpose for me. Simply put, music was Laurie and Phil's *Why* and it became my *Why* as well - the very core of my being. It's what drives me and helps me to be the person I am meant to be. Inspiring others by composing and performing meaningful music energizes me like nothing else. What is it for you? Have you thought about what your *Why* is? There is power behind *Why* we do what we do, and I encourage you to define what that is for you.

Backtracking a little, Laurie and I were blessed with parents who loved us, but who didn't truly love each other, and at times there was certainly tension in our home. At the time I wasn't aware, but looking back, one of the ways I coped with this was playing piano and trumpet for several hours each day. It helped that our parents were both musical and made the investment in private lessons. My private teachers became more than just people I learned piano or trumpet from. They taught me about life, and they showed me possibilities I could have never other-wise imagined. What a gift. They truly exhibited their *Why* in their own lives, and I learned from their examples. It became apparent to me that anything was possible, if I used my God-given gifts to their full potential.

There's more to the story. The summer after my parents' divorce, I practiced piano five hours per day, missing only one day all summer. Our piano sounded atrocious and was frus-trating to play, so my father finally called the piano technician to come do his magic. The technician also happened to have been my 7th grade band director, so we already had a good rapport, and he knew I had a keen ear for pitch. At that tuning appointment, he also learned I had excellent mechanical apti-tude, and showed me how to make some adjustments to the piano action. While I was making one such adjustment on all eighty-eight notes, he and my father enjoyed some coffee in the kitchen. Little did I know what they were up to, but a few months later, on my sixteenth birthday, my father gave me a set of piano tuning tools and a book on how to tune and service pianos. Though I couldn't see it at the time, this would become yet another *Why* – another gift in my life.

Tuning pianos led me to meet some of my best friends and acquaintances, which also led to many other opportunities, including doing professional concert recording and sound for orchestras, bands, and choral ensembles in Southeast Wisconsin. These experiences have inspired me to compose and record my own music, which has now become my greatest purpose – my greatest *Why*: 'To inspire, encourage, lead, and give others hope through my music, words, and enthusiasm.' I revisit my mission statement often, to make sure I'm still on track. Do you have a mission statement? If not, I hope this story has helped to inspire you to write your own mission statement - the *Why* behind everything you do.

I feel the need to tell you about my first piano teacher, Ruth Schoening. She was also our church organist, and always encouraged me to play with her during the service, and sub for her in her absence. She's now ninety-six years young and still plays piano at her retirement home. And her encouragement stays with me to this day as I play piano and organ for my own church. One of the greatest blessings I continually experience is playing for funerals. Hearing all the stories of how people have lived their lives so fully, truly living out their *Why* in such meaningful ways, has had a massive impact on how I try to live my life. I am thankful that God has chosen this path for my life, and consequently, many countless blessings have come my way.

So, back to the *Wishing Well* – how does the story end? Does the little girl's wish come true? Well, in the original version of the song it's somewhat ambiguous, with the girl always holding hope that her parents can make things right, but Laurie and Phil did eventually rewrite the song to have a happy ending. This meaningful song has stayed with me all these years, and thirty years later, I've finally released my first solo piano album entitled *Journey Home* with my own arrangement of *Wishing Well*. It's the only song on the album I didn't write, but it's one of my favorites, and now you know the true meaning behind the song. I hope you'll go download the audio recording of *Wishing Well* for free on my website, listed below. At the check-out, use the discount code FreeSingle.

Throughout my life, all these various threads have woven the tapestry of my *Power of Why*, and it is my hope that I can inspire others to also live with great purpose. Let your *Power of Why* turn Adversity into Advantage, Stress into Strength, and Pain into Passion. Blessings on your journey.

Author Bio:

Eric Carlson is a Wisconsin-born composer and pianist. A classically trained musician, Eric is principal keyboardist for The Racine Symphony Orchestra, a Registered Piano Technician and Sales Manager for Artistic Piano Service, and a recording engineer.

https://EricCarlsonPiano.com

15

TO COMPOSE

John Burge
Canada

T welve Riffs on Why I Became a Composer

1. Because my parents gave me the gift of music. This is a box that remains expansively bottomless to this day.

2. Because I sat at the piano at an early age and learned that improvisation is just finding a few notes and making them behave in ways that are both spontaneous and inevitable. I also realized that it is often best not to worry too much about writing everything down at first as the mind will eventually isolate the most important kernels if given the chance. The trick here, and this only comes with practice, is to learn to iden-tify a kernel that is strong enough to bear the weight of the music's finished form.

3. Because, as Schoenberg said, "There is still plenty of music left to be written in C Major." At different times I inter-

pret these words to convey a sense of challenge, an element of regret, or simply a statement of reality. Perhaps it is sufficient to say that the world is vast and there exists the capacity to continually tell the same stories differently.

4. Because my father's library had some great volumes of piano music. Slowly playing music far beyond one's technical ability is a great way to learn how to sight read while simultaneously instilling elements of compositional craft that can last a lifetime.

5. Because in grade nine I broke my left leg skiing. Lying on my back and looking at my leg hanging ninety degrees askew, I still remember thinking that at least I could still use my right foot to manipulate the piano's damper pedal. Perhaps this was the moment of no turning back from a career in music. Later, seated at a piano for the first time following eighteen days in hospital, I can still recall how comforting the keyboard felt when touching the keys. Having a full leg cast for over four months inevitably led to sitting for hours at the keyboard. This kind of enforced dedication and endurance is the fodder upon which careers are often made.

6. Because being a composer creates sympathetic reverberations with other forms of artistic expression such that the time spent appreciating other spheres of creativity will inevitably unlock sources of unexpected inspiration in your own art. Simply put, as a composer, the things you are drawn to and admire will always find ways to be expressed in your music. Like all creative pursuits, composing, when approached with conviction, love and honesty, becomes as easy as breathing. It is not work at all, but a calling. In my own case, I am continually drawn to finding a musical springboard in the landscape and images of Canada. Equally, using music to capture the shading of a poem's meaning has instilled a lifelong love of poetry that continually primes the floodgates. [As Exhibit A, consider how Anne Michaels's

poem, *To Write*, has influenced the approach taken to structure these reflections.]

7. Because Dorothy Hare taught me how to be the best
pianist I could be. A composer who has some professional
ability as a singer or instrumentalist will invariably work
productively and collegially with performers. With great peda-
gogical imagination, Dorothy attempted to slow down my vora-
cious appetite to learn new music by imposing a rule that I
could only read from the score of a new piece for one lesson.
Thereafter, the composition or movement had to be played
from memory, polished to an acceptable level, and then ideally
performed a few times in public before new repertoire was
added. Being able to mentally carry a very exacting image of a
composition in your mind, and to perform confidently from
memory in public, are abilities I continually rely upon. By
extension, I have learned to fill my idle thoughts while doing
such mindless activities as running or trying to fall asleep, with
the mental reworking of notes, chords, and broader composition concepts. Surprisingly, this is often when the big creative
problems get solved.

8. Because I was blessed with meeting the love of my life in
a high school orchestra. Not only did we get married when I
was just twenty-one, but I found a partner who can be counted
on for constant support and keenest criticism. Having one
person embody both a soulmate and sounding board has
smoothed out many bumps along the way.

9. Because Michael Klazek, a high school music teacher, not
only had the school orchestra play my compositions, but he
taught me how to copy music professionally with pen and ink.
Anyone under about the age of fifty will find the idea of striving
to become a competent music copyist incredibly hard to believe
—but then I am old enough to have never used a computer
during any of my university course work.

10. Because I probably wasn't smart enough to do anything

else. Basically, I was willing to do whatever it took to fashion a career where writing music was a priority. Put another way, I didn't have an alternate career path to pursue if I couldn't turn my composer dream into a reality. Thankfully, some wonderful composition professors at the University of Toronto and University of British Columbia pointed me in the right direction. There are so many potential setbacks in attempting to become a creative artist in any field and not having an escape route likely means that your art will be given the chance to grow and eventually prosper.

11. Because so many great musicians and conductors took the time to program, commission, and perform my music. As the saying goes, "Nothing breeds success, like success." Truly though, to hear your own music performed beautifully in public is to experience a kind of euphoria that is as close as I get to imagining a heaven on earth.

12. Because the twelve chromatic pitches of the tonal system, and by extension the twenty-four major and minor keys, exist in orbits that are constantly changing and open to new interpretations and procedures. The shifting relationship between pitches, chords, and keys, continually creates new compositional opportunities, moving at times with supple elasticity, heightened intensity or startling surprise. Bach, Chopin, Shostakovich, and Buczynski—to name but four composers who systematically explored all twenty-four major and minor keys—can't be wrong. Further though, the potential to have a composition defined not by its tonality or harmony, but by a prominent emphasis on such things as rhythm, texture or instrumental colour, continually opens new paths for a composer to explore. What could be more inspiring?

Author Bio:

A Juno-winning composer, John Burge has taught at Queen's University, Canada, since 1987. Recognized for his arts leadership, he has served on many boards including being the longest-serving President of the Canadian League of Composers.

https://johnburge.ca/page

16

HOW COMPOSITION SAVED ME

David A. Jones
United Kingdom

The story of how I survived my earliest piano lessons and through simple discoveries, achieved my musical dreams.

But first, consider this:

Music looks like it sounds, it sounds like it feels, and it feels like it looks.

Applying that thought to the piano, the notation of a typical ascending major scale shows evenly rising notes (how it looks = visual). We hear the music go up in pitch as we play (how it sounds = aural). We feel our fingers rise up the keyboard (how it feels = kinesthetic).

Now add the rhythmic component. When notation is correctly, proportionally spaced, the visual pattern of the rhythms directly correlate to their performance in time. Therefore, three basic components of music - aural, visual and kinesthetic - link directly to our three main learning styles.

Notation is just a graphic representation of where and

when to play. We humans are mostly a pattern-loving species. If we recognise the shapes within music, we progress quicker. There are a few of us who learn a little differently, but shapes and patterns are how we learn intuitively from our earliest days.

Some musicians will hear those patterns more easily, some need to feel them first, others will need to read them, as they slowly link the three together on their learning journey. Who is to say that any of these learning styles is more important than another?

Next, imagine giving a child paint, brushes, and paper but only letting them copy existing paintings, telling them that they must paint exactly the same as the original otherwise it is wrong. What an awful thought.

Seeing the genius creative artwork that comes straight from a child's mind or hearing their first experimental composition is magical. Allowing a student free play on an instrument (being careful of course) is their artistic expression being heard. Therefore, should composition not be a natural part of music lessons from day one?

Finally, before my story, I have a philosophy about composition:

Imagine every piece of music you have ever heard, from music you actively enjoy, through all the music you passively absorb, including that song you heard on holiday that you loved but never found again. Your Musical Input is as unique to you as your fingerprint.

That Musical Input shapes our musical preferences as we write. At each point on the fluid path of composition, decisions are made - consciously or not - as to what turns to make in the melody, harmony, arrangement etc. We can't really have a strong, emotional affinity to music we haven't heard yet, though that is not to say that we can't aim to write music that pushes new boundaries.

No one else will shape those unique influences like you. No one else will write your music, and as you are in charge, it can't be wrong. In time, we'll refine our compositional craft so we will like more of what we create. By learning the so-called 'rules' of composition, we understand why we like what we do, so we can write what we want.

Composing shows me where I have come from musically and how it influences my output via my own creative spin. I feel I am writing the story of my continuing learning curve. Everything I've absorbed helps to shape my writing. In turn, maybe it shows where I am going.

As I work in both Music Education and Production, I feel I am composing a legacy for my children to look back on - a journey of me aiming to do a cool thing - to help music students of all levels, from complete beginners to advanced, discover, grow and express themselves in a way that music saved me.

Here's that story:

I started formal piano lessons aged eight with a teacher I had for just a year. On day one, I was shown all the notes on lines and spaces plus two ledger lines above and below the Grand Stave - I still have the book to prove this. Though I have personal opinions on the pedagogy and practicality of teaching an eight-year-old this material in lesson one, let's just say for now that this did not suit my learning style.

My sight reading didn't improve much at first. As written notation was the sole device around which my lessons revolved, I was indoctrinated into the idea that this was the only way to learn and anything else was a poor imitation. I began to feel like a second-rate student.

Yet I still loved the sound of the piano and how the notes would blend together. I soon got tired of playing other people's music, so I started experimenting. This truly set off a spark. I started improvising at home with simple tunes, but it was chord sequences that really moved me. I was enthralled by the moods conjured up through harmonic progressions.

As I was developing my aural and composition skills, I felt guilty. I thought this was holding my reading back even further. However, I was simply developing quickly through my preferred learning style. If I'd been forced to read and read only, I would have given up years before, through sheer frustration. Soon, I was starting to compose material of a higher level than I was playing in my lessons.

I started to write out my piano pieces which drew me into learning more about Music Theory. If I was going to take the time to notate my music, I was going to get it right and so the link to written music was made. As soon as I started to write what I had played, I literally saw and understood what I could feel and hear. I'd faltered through the early years, but I began to incorporate what my next few teachers taught me with my own personal discoveries via aural and kinesthetic learning. In turn, I'd begun to unlock the written music too.

The route to achieving my musical goals came through discovering that there is more than one way to learn music. All learning styles are valid, and they are all correct.

In a world where so much needs to be changed for the better, I feel I might have the most impact in helping others find and express themselves through music. In doing so, we discover more about who we are. Maybe we'll learn more about others too. I'm certainly not trying to say that composing will fix all our troubles, but music certainly has the power to bring people together, singing in one voice, both literally and metaphorically.

Author Bio:

David A Jones (BAPMR): Director of Presto Music School, Award-Winning Film Composer, Co-Creator of the Musical TV Series *Rhythm Warriors* produced by Emofront and Presto Music Production in association with Sparky Animation Studios.

www.prestomusicschool.co.uk

17

SONGS OF HOPE

Julianne Warkentin
Canada

If you would have met me when I was six years old, you would have assumed I had a perfect childhood. I had a loving family, a beautiful home in a small town, and had many opportunities. But hidden behind my smile and blonde curls were dark memories I buried since they were too painful for me to deal with.

One of my first memories in my life was witnessing my older brother's shocking and tragic accident. At his funeral, I was too young to really understand what had happened. I remember nervously playing with the buttons on my coat while my family and I stared at Frankie's coffin in a state of frozen sadness. It was too awful to be real since he was only seven and the only boy in the family. My father endured the unbearable agony of blaming himself for the accident, so we all carried on in a fog of silent grief.

Since my parents were suffering and overwhelmed, I was often put in the care of friends and relatives. These were people that immigrated to Canada from Europe together with my parents to escape the second world war. Some of them were very kind but others were cruel and abusive to me. They were wolves in sheep's clothing and the deep betrayal was heartbreaking and traumatic. I was far too terrified to consider telling anyone what was happening to me especially considering the threats that were clearly communicated. Even worse, I feared no one would believe me.

Although the abuse finally stopped by the time I was seven, the damage was done, and I couldn't shake the shameful feeling that it must have been my fault. Why else would these friends hurt me? Sadly, my beautiful German Shepherd Sambi was the only one that seemed to understand how scared and lonely I was and continually got in trouble for growling at my enemies.

At such a tender age, it became obvious to me that life was a battle between good and evil. I saw that even though life could be cruel, hope was present along my journey: my sweet mother, cherished pets, my kind piano teacher, my faith, and my music stand out as songs of hope for my wounded heart.

Although my mother, Ruth, didn't like to talk about feelings, she was a consistently loving presence in my life. I have no doubt I would not have survived without her. I knew my father Frank loved me too, but he coped with his grief by being aloof and extremely busy. The times he did show affection to me growing up are very precious but few. I am so thankful that we grew close when I was an adult.

My faith turned out to be an anchor of hope for my soul. From an early age, my mom taught me that I was a beloved child of God and that there was a divine purpose for my life. While I cuddled on her lap, she often would read to me the story of Joseph in the Old Testament that I identified with. His life started with abuse and betrayal, but he trusted God to help him and bless his future. He blossomed in his abilities and talents as he grew older. I believed with all my heart that this miracle could happen to me too.

My first memory of music in my life was my mother singing to me at bedtime. I still remember the words of some of the songs she sang about birds, flowers, angels, and stars - songs of hope and freedom.

Music was also a wonderful part of my family both at home and in my little country church in the woods. It brought much needed joy to my family's heavy hearts. My sisters filled our house with piano music, and I adored listening to *The Sound of Music* on our record player. My father and I listened to the beauty of Mozart while driving his shiny Chrysler. When my Oma came to visit, she would watch *Hymn Sing* on our black and white television while adding her rich alto voice.

I started piano lessons when I was seven, and the piano soon became a magical world of music I could escape to. My kind and encouraging piano teacher was Mrs. Frances Funk. I remember driving with my mom along Crescent Lake to her pretty blue house surrounded by very tall trees. For many years, she patiently taught me theory and piano skills that helped me excel in piano and discover my ability for composing and love for teaching. During summer holidays, I was gathering neighborhood children to teach them uplifting songs I had learned from her and my mom. I loved pretending I was a music teacher.

I remember making up simple songs and stories at an early age. When I was around nine, I began composing music for special occasions and to express my emotions. I learned how to compose by studying the music of composers that I loved. Composing became the language of my heart, and I could say anything I felt or imagined on the piano keys.

As an adult, composing was an emotional and spiritual outlet for me but also a way of reclaiming childhood joy I had missed out on. Composing humorous and entertaining songs about animals, pets, and children's adventures was what my heart needed. My own children and students loved these piano solos which added to the fun.

As a teacher, composer, wife, and mother, I am so grateful for the kind people that graced my life with hope. There were caring friends, the supportive love of my children and husband Brad, professional therapists and counselors, spiritual mentors, support groups, and those who guided me to meaningful volunteer work. I also appreciate my early start as a published composer thanks to the Associated Manitoba Art's Festival and the Canadian National Conservatory of Music.

My dream has always been to bring hope to others through my job, gifts, and talents. My healing came from finding purpose in my pain. I once felt hopeless and discouraged so I have desperately wanted to bring hope and encouragement to others. Slowly through many struggles over many years, my wounded heart has transformed from just surviving to thriving. I learned that I could be someone that could bring 'songs of hope' to the life of another - just like others had done for me.

Author Bio:

Julianne Warkentin is a creative Canadian composer, inspiring teacher, festival adjudicator, theory specialist, performer and presenter. Along with her ARCT in piano performance from Toronto's Royal Conservatory of music, she is a member of the Manitoba registered usic Teachers' Association. Her music is inspired by her spiritual journey and nature.

Instagram: Julianne.piano

18

MUSIC COMPOSITION: MORE THAN A HOBBY

Hillary Lester
United States

I didn't write a single piece of music until I was nineteen. While I grew up in a musical family, sang in choirs, played piano, flute, and guitar, it never occurred to me that I could write classical music professionally. My rural Montana community was heavily rooted in the sciences, and in the eyes of most of my teachers, it was 'just a hobby'.

When I graduated high school, I did what any other sensible and confused eighteen-year-old with a penchant for the sciences would do - I enrolled at a local university to study engineering. Everything looked good on paper: I had perfect grades, a full ride with scholarships, and my professors saw great potential in me. The only problem was I became massively depressed.

I had this horrible feeling I couldn't explain. I spent my nights listening to music thinking, "I miss this. I wish I could just do this." I spent my free time researching music programs, anything to get me out of engineering. And that's when I found it - a music composition degree at a state university just a few hours down the road. That unexplainable feeling came back, this time with a warning, "go back into music or you'll continue down this dark road of depression."

Not really knowing what I was getting myself into, I transferred universities and enrolled in the music department. I received criticism at every step from my professors, my friends, and my dad, who was an engineer. Despite being told that it was an easy worthless degree, I went from perfect grades in engineering to failing my theory placement exam and my first choir audition. I was so out of my element and scared that I wanted to give up and go back that first week. But I had great support from my family (even my dad came around), and after taking my first composition class, by all miracles, my gut was right: I felt like I was home.

It wasn't that music magically cured the depression in my life. Rather, I found a deeper meaning for my life and an avenue to feel my emotions. I could express myself in ways I never felt were possible in the sciences. Studying music at the collegiate level evoked emotions and a sense of joy that was deep, often unexplainable, and profound.

When I was in school, everything made sense. Singing in two choirs, working on multiple composition projects, hearing magic take place in the concert halls, and preparing for voice lessons all gave meaning to my life. However, the moment I graduated, the bottom fell out. I had no training and no mentor to prepare me for how far I would fall from the safety of the university. I scrambled to find musical work in Montana, but the opportunities I imagined and realized for myself were next to nothing.

After two years of working day jobs and longing to return to music, that gut feeling in my life showed up again, loud as ever. I felt called to go back into music overseas and enrolled in a summer program in Paris and a master's program in Birmingham, England. My time in Europe was wonderful. I experienced a culture of music completely different from my home. Music wasn't 'just a hobby,' it was life and a respectable, noble career to pursue.

When I graduated with my master's in composition, I felt like I was on top of the world. However, the moment I moved home, my mental health crumbled yet again. This time I was determined to find a way to keep music alive in my life. But as a classical composer living in Montana, I had no idea where to start.

While music was a great avenue for my mental health, I realized that whenever I wasn't practicing music, I couldn't keep my spirits up. That led me on a journey to discover wellness using non-musical modalities. I got into lifting weights, following exercise programs, practicing yoga, reading personal development books, and meditating. It completely changed my life, and for the first time outside of music, I was thriving mentally.

Then something unexpected happened. The more I healed myself, the more creative I got with ideas on how to build a musical practice in my life in Montana. In July of 2020, I founded *The Healthy Musician Site* and started blogging on my experiences. Since then, I've had dozens of people tell me how much sharing my stories meant to them and that I wasn't alone in those struggles. After seeing so many of my posts, I was approached by an old colleague of mine to cohost a podcast to interview musicians from around the world. *The Sounds of the World* podcast was born and helped me further network and connect in ways I never imagined were possible.

In January 2021, one of those gut feelings struck again. Only this time I wasn't called to return to music, I felt called to help other musicians thrive by developing their own wellness practices. In June 2021, I ran my first virtual wellness summit for musicians and the results for the participants were nothing short of amazing.

My journey in composition connected me with so many amazing people, but most of all, it helped me connect with myself. Studying and composing music allowed me to travel, find many perspectives outside of myself, and begin healing on a deep transformational level. Although I'm not as active in writing music as I once was, I find great meaning in connecting with other musicians, raising awareness on our mental health, and shedding light on common musical struggles.

I've never once regretted choosing music composition instead of engineering. It's opened so many worlds for me, and, most of all, allowed me to bring healing to my little world here in Montana. Music isn't 'just a hobby.' For me, it's the only thing that makes sense.

Author Bio:

Hillary Lester is a life coach for musicians and an American contemporary composer. She holds an MA (Music) from University of Birmingham (UK) and a BM (Music Composition) from the University of Montana (US).

http://thehealthymusiciansite.com/

19

I WILL NEVER BE GOOD ENOUGH

Joanne Barker
Canada

'I will never be good enough.' That phrase has been repeated in my head and in my heart throughout my life.

As a child, I was tiny for my age, which according to some, made me weak. I was definitely not 'good enough' to do many things others were able to do. Being born third of four in a blue-collar family definitely came with challenges. We had one car, our father worked long hours, and money was tight, so extracurricular activities were limited to what was available in our village. We enrolled in figure skating lessons at the local arena, thanks to a family discount.

While I loved skating, I was painfully aware that many were better than I could ever hope to be. There was a good reason why I could not skate a clean edge, but I would not learn why until many years later. Still, I loved skating as I was able to be in a new environment, surrounded by music.

At age nine, I started taking piano lessons from our neighbor. Piano quickly became the center of my world. After only six months of lessons, I won an audition and gave my first performance for an audience of over 400 people. I can still remember the feeling of the applause. In that moment, I felt more than good enough; I felt so alive. That performance began a life filled with countless public performances at school, church, and community events.

I loved performing but still felt that I was not good enough. After all, we only had an old upright piano in the basement, not a grand piano in the living room. My teacher was my neighbor, not a member of a prestigious conservatory. Still, when I was playing, nothing else mattered. I loved making up tunes, adding harmonies, and experimenting with rhythms.

When I was in Grade 8, the new music teacher at our school produced a musical in which I was cast in the elite chorus. Soon I was playing many of the songs on the piano and adding my own accompaniments. During a break in practice one day, the teacher walked back into the room to find me playing the piano, as my cast mates danced and sang along. From the look on her face, I thought I had done something wrong. Apparently, I had not. After that day, I became the rehearsal pianist.

At age eighteen, she asked me to become the official accompanist for the school choirs. For the next ten years, I had the privilege of working with an award winning, demanding woman who had very high standards. She taught me about performing and how to make more of the music on the page. I soon learned how to improvise and create on my own. Working for her was a huge boost in my self-confidence and creativity.

At age nineteen, I won a coveted spot in a university music program without ever having taken a piano exam. I was sure that a music degree would make me feel 'good enough'. I was surrounded with high achieving, skilled classmates who inspired me to work hard. My first year was a success, but I struggled with feeling that I was not good enough to be there.

During my first year at university, the reason for those less than perfect figure skating edges was revealed. Exploratory surgery determined that my right knee required reconstructive surgery to correct a misalignment. Following surgery, a pinched nerve caused drop foot. I then had a fall which resulted in a torn ankle ligament. The need for extensive physiotherapy meant that continuing full time studies was not possible. My goal of achieving a Bachelor of Music was gone. How would I ever feel that I was good enough without that degree?

Thankfully, my university piano professor agreed to keep me on as a private student. Under her guidance, I successfully completed the Grade 10 Piano exam which meant I could start work on my new goal of achieving the Associate Degree in Piano.

Physical issues continued to plague me. I was diagnosed with tendonitis and carpal tunnel syndrome in both wrists. I was left unable to play for extended periods of time, so I would not be able to put in enough practice time to achieve the level of performance required for the exam. The news was devastating. My goal of completing the Associate exam was gone. I again faced the awful feeling that I would never be good enough.

I had started teaching piano and had a dedicated group of students. I decided I would become the best piano teacher I could be. I attended teacher workshops, searching for student materials, and learning about the latest teaching trends. I was constantly revising and changing the music in the lesson materials that I was using for my students. Even after exhaustive searching, I could not find material that I felt fulfilled what I wanted for my students.

My teaching career flourished when I started offering group piano lessons. Eventually, my lesson structure evolved into a hybrid system of group plus private lessons, but I was still not happy with any material that was commercially available.

It was at this time that I was diagnosed with breast cancer.

Cancer brought my world to a halt. Somehow, I made it through that difficult year and emerged ready to face the world with even more joy. About a year after treatment ended, I had an ah-ha moment. Why not compose my own lesson materials? But wait, I am not a composer. I do not have a music degree. I have never been taught how to compose. As I thought about it, I realized that I have been arranging and creating music ever since I started playing piano. I had written many pieces, but did that make me a composer?

Perhaps there is more to being a composer than being told you are 'good enough'. Perhaps it is up to each of us to decide for ourselves that what we are creating is worthy, and not look for that affirmation from others. Nothing gives me more joy than when a student asks to play their favourite piece - and that piece turns out to be one of my compositions. Those moments fill my heart.

Why do I compose? The reason is simple – I want lesson materials for my students. The by-product of my efforts far outweighs the reason why I do it. I have finally proven to myself that I am indeed 'good enough'.

Author Bio:

Joanne Barker, UMTC Elite Educator, Piano Teacher, Composer, UMT Creative Designer. Joanne has created a hybrid lesson system combining group piano with private instruction. She has composed or arranged the beginner and intermediate lesson materials used in her studio.

https://ultimatemusictheory.com/about-ultimate-music-theory/

20

WHAT'S IN A NAME

Richard Simonelli
United States

M e: I'm Richie Simonelli from the Bronx, New York, and
I write country music songs.

Sony Music Nashville: Are you a full-time writer?

Me: No, I have a full-time job on Wall Street, but I want to
be a songwriter.

Sony Music Nashville: We aren't looking for new music
right now, but keep on writing.

Me: Honey, I'm on my way home."

I thought country music was my ticket to stardom and I
couldn't believe that Nashville wasn't ready for Richie
Simonelli.

The year was 1994 and country music was sweeping America. The rock-n-roll influenced Garth Brooks (born two days
after me in 1962) had first taken over country music and then all
of America with an energy and talent for ripping fast songs,
telling great stories, and the sincerity of delivering truly great
ballads. He sold tens of millions of records at a time and played

to sold out football stadiums. He was massive before he stopped cold and *retired* to take time off to be with his wife and kids.

As for me, I was thirty-two and still wanted to make it in music after taking the safe route laid out by my parents: going to school, getting a job, getting married, having kids, and moving to the suburbs. I was living out a Jimmy Buffet song and it wasn't *Margaritaville*. Instead, I figuratively "died and moved to the suburbs and was having puppies, raising yuppies".

But country music was where it was at and where I wanted to be. It was rock with a fiddle and steel guitar. The lyrics mattered, and you could actually understand the singer. And you could dance. In fact, we all got up to dance. There were literally lines to get into line dancing clubs in New York City, and I was playing in bars all over New York with a country cover band.

"In the face of my rejection, I looked up to see, the humbled reflection of the Man I Used to Be." -from the song "The Man I Used to Be" by JD Tucker.

After that terrible trip to Nashville, I went back home and immediately wrote an album's worth of some really good songs. The great thing about rejection is that you always get great songs from it. *Greetings from Nashville, The Waffle House Song, Ballerina* and the one that almost made it into the movie *Grumpy Old Men* starring Jack Lemmon & Walter Matthau. The song was called *Take Your Tongue Out My Mouth Cos' I'm Kissing you Goodbye*- Thank God that didn't happen. Imagine if that was the only song I was known for.

I recorded my new songs for a new album with a producer friend of mine, Terry Fabrizio. He is an amazing guitar player and has been a top arranger and producer for decades. Everybody loves him and as a result, he knows everybody on the New York music scene. Terry said, "These songs sound like the

Eagles." So, Terry brought in a killer backing vocalist Margaret Dorn with amazing range and tons of Nashville credits. He also brought in an uber talented multi-instrumentalist who could play fiddle, mandolin, and steel guitar, Larry Campbell. Larry would go on to be a major player with Bob Dylan, Cyndi Lauper, and he even became the lead guitarist and musical director for Levon Helm. Larry has even won a few Grammys.

When the album was finished, I was determined to go back to Nashville. But this time as an artist, not a songwriter. And like one of my idols, Elton John, I needed a new name, a country name. Richie from the Bronx wasn't going to cut it.

I ended up becoming JD Tucker. JD for my maternal grand-father Jerry Desmond, a piano player from 1950's New York and Tucker, who was my dog. I couldn't wait to get on David Letterman and tell him how I got such a cool name. "Well Dave, a lot of people think the JD stands for Jack Daniels Whiskey...."

On my next trip to Nashville as JD Tucker, I was welcomed on Music Row, returning like the prodigal son. I knew someone who set me up with a dozen meetings with Nashville execs and they listened to three songs each off the record. I heard the same thing over and over from multiple people.

"These are great recordings; the guy on pedal steel is amazing. I don't hear a single, but I am impressed with your song-writing. You got it kid."

I was flattered, but I didn't hear the line I wanted to hear. "We want to sign you to a record deal." Instead, they wanted to sign me as a songwriter. Several times I heard: "Our writers make $150 a week to start and write from 9-5pm. You get to write with all kinds of folks, and over the years, our writers build up royalties from getting tracks on albums. The good ones make a lot of money. We think you could be a good one."

I was making $150,000 a year on Wall Street with a young family and Tucker, our dog. The decision was really easy for me.

"Reach for the stars but remember who you are." - from the song *Always Be Yourself* by JD Tucker

I bet you are reading this waiting to see that I quit that job, moved to Nashville and wrote a bunch of number one hits for other artists. But I chose the kids and the dog. I am doing the reverse Garth Brooks. I focused first on the kids, music second.

I am JD Tucker, and I have never stopped writing and recording. I have written over a hundred songs and have a bunch of albums on iTunes. I have my own recording studio. I am still working with Terry Fabrizio, and we are in the studio currently working on the next JD Tucker album.

Stay tuned. The stadium tours are next.

Author Bio:

Richard Simonelli aka JD Tucker, is a singer-songwriter composer living by the Chesapeake Bay, USA with his two angels: his wife Angela and dog Angel. His two daughters, Adrianna and Nicole, are all grown up and wonderful.

www.jdtucker.com

21

JUST DO IT

Gillian Erskine
Australia

I'd love to say that it was like Mozart or Beethoven and that I
have music endlessly playing in my head that I just have to
write down. The truth is far more realistic. I started composing
from necessity. Yes, rather than a driving desire to express my
innermost thoughts and feelings on paper, I began composing
simply because I needed to. As one of the world's most famous
sporting brands says, rather than fiddling and fussing about
when the need arises... "Just do it."

They say necessity is the mother of all inventions and that's
exactly where I found myself as a first-time composer along
with Paul Myatt, best friend, and business partner of more than
twenty-seven years, as we were about to launch our *Forte School
of Music* system.

Sure, I'd done some arranging in my time. Over the years,
I'd taught state champions and national finalists for electronic
organ festivals. Competition was always fierce, with top-quality
performances. Artistry was high, and we worked for months on

crafting arrangements, not to mention programming rhythms and choreographing registrations (sound combinations). I was used to solving puzzles and finding creative solutions but composing, other than the odd rift, bridge passage, variation or cadenza, was new to me.

Cycle forward to the summer of 1993-1994 when we decided to launch our own music education system. There was a ton of work to do, most importantly, having course materials ready for some 2000 students. The new school year was looming.

We had designed our course overview and had already included a variety of musical styles and genres from traditional songs, arrangements of popular classics, and standard piano repertoire. What we needed now was some extra pedagogically crafted compositions to fit into our course progression like a glove.

The magic was going to be in having extra pieces in a contemporary style that sounded good, kids were going to be excited by, enjoy playing, and were easy to teach.

We knew the specific job each new piece had to do and with the absence of both time and money, the decision was simple. We had to compose these pieces ourselves.

I had mixed feelings. I remember feeling daunted and yet excited. At times I felt blank, like when someone says, "Draw me a picture," and you find yourself staring at a piece of paper waiting for creative inspiration. I felt overwhelmed, with thoughts like, "Where do I start?", "What do I write?" not to mention Miss Imposter who asked, "Can I even do this?"

I was suffering from every block you could imagine, writer's block, composer's block, and imagination block. Then it came to me, I just needed to create specific pieces to do a specific job. This was a blessing as my inspiration need only be a chord progression, a note range, an interval, or technical element. Something to provide a focus point can offer that genesis of inspiration.

Long story short, we cobbled together enough material to launch that summer. Each book was like having a baby, but the labyrinth was in the nine months not the end. I remember the excitement each time we opened the first box of newly printed course books. It was amazing to see our creation in real life. Necessity led to us creating a curriculum of four courses with nineteen books that enabled our Forte Schools to cater for children from four years through to middle school.

After a few years, there was increasing demand from parents of even younger children in the early childhood naught-three- year-old sector. After searching for an ideal course, I realised that I had to dust off my composing chops and head the writing team to develop *Jungle Music*, our early childhood program.

Most early childhood programs use traditional music, presented in a simple way. We recognised the importance of that, but we had a vision for something a little different. We wanted music that would engage and appeal to parents. Music they would be eager to share with their children. The music still needed to be simple and easily understood by this young age group, yet we wanted to inject an element of youth and vitality that was new to children's educational music. It was a proud moment when in 2004 we won an Australian-made award for this course.

Over the years we have continued to write both original pieces and arrangements, many of which have been published by giants Warner Chappell & Alfred Publishing. In 1997, the first of our *easiLEARN Theory Fundamentals* books was released. Using a puzzle book approach means kids don't even realise they are learning theory. The six-book series is available in Australia, UK and soon North America.

Over the past two years, we've returned to the blank manuscript: writing, arranging, and editing for the *Discovering Piano* series for Beginners to Early Advanced in the Piano

Teaching Success members-only community, The Studio. Necessity continues to be the key theme.

Like an author with writer's block, I still struggle to get my head into the space of writing. It often takes Paul's instigation, but I must say I really do love our composing days. It's like visiting a beautiful art gallery. My brain switches gears and rustles out the cobwebs. I find myself just playing and playing, looking for the gems of ideas as a piece comes together under my hands. I think about the patterns and the way they feel. So, I just play and play until the magic clicks into place.

For me, composing is like opening a secret chamber with one of those ancient keys that you'd see in a movie. Each little notch has to click into place and only then will the secret door open. This is the feeling I get when a new piece or arrangement comes together. I love that feeling of calm and peace that happens when, like the dawning of a new day, the door opens, and I know we're done.

As I look back on what has been twenty-five plus years of composing on and off and the legacy Paul and I have created, I am grateful that life took these twists and turns which forced me to do things I wouldn't have imagined.

When opportunity calls on you to dig deep and go on an unexpected adventure, remember life has a way of presenting us with the most extraordinary opportunities. Who are we to not take them up?

So, when life presents you with an extraordinary opportunity...
Just do it.

Author Bio:

Gillian Erskine is the CEO of Forte School of Music and Piano Teaching Success. Gillian's passion is to help others make learning music fun, so more children go on to enjoy the lifelong pleasure of playing music.

www.pianoteachingsuccess.com

22

JOY COMES WITH THE MORNING

Rick Sowash
United States

I magine that we're standing near a bramble of wild blackberry bushes, you and me. If I pick a blackberry and pop, it in my mouth, chew it up and swallow it, then that blackberry is ... a certain kind of thing. Bear with me here.

Now, suppose I picked that same blackberry and said to you, "Hey, will you pay me a nickel for this blackberry?" The glistening little fruit has now become a different thing than it was in the previous instance. It looks the same, smells the same, tastes the same. It has the same name. Nevertheless, it has changed. Spiritually, it has become something else. Through no fault of its own, it has been diminished.

Trying to sell a blackberry which came to us for free changes the blackberry, our relationship to it and our relationship with one another. Not for the better.

The attempt to sell something alters the thing that is being offered for sale as well as the friendship and mutual trust that may exist between the potential seller and the prospective buyer. This is especially true when both parties know that the thing being offered came to the seller for free.

Ideas, blackberries, morning, joy, and a great many other good things come to us for free. The universe provides them. They offset weeping.

From Psalm 30: "Weeping may tarry for the night, but joy comes with the morning."

Every Sunday morning, I send an email offering a little story, an mp3 of my music, and a pdf of the score to about 650 friends and fans.

Lately, I've been thinking, though I could not have foreseen it, the sharing of these emails was the goal of my career all along.

For fifty years, I wrote music, always with a vague notion that sooner or later, somewhere or other, it would be performed, would be heard, would mean something to someone. I anticipated that my music would be heard in recitals, concerts, worship services, and broadcasts... and it was.

In October 2013, only because I thought it would be fun, I began sending a Sunday morning email to friends and fans. From the start, I included a vignette, a 'back story' or a mini-essay, sometimes humorous, sometimes thoughtful.

Then and now, I enjoyed doing the writing and enjoyed when friends responded. Fun, indeed.

Then, in 2019, came the pandemic. Overnight, the purpose, meaning and impact of these emails deepened. Deprived of concerts, recitals, worship services, and each other's company, our email inboxes assumed a new importance.

The practice of writing and sharing these emails has reshaped my notion of what I was doing when I was composing all that music and trying to get it 'out there.'

Without knowing it, I was preparing to be in a position to send out these 'e-pistles' as gestures of friendship during the worst year in living memory.

Getting to the point that I could do such a thing was a lengthy, expensive, and complicated process. Until 1995, all my scores were hand-written. I had to master a computer music notation program so that I could share professional-looking scores in pdf form; I hired a graduate student to tutor me. I had to recruit musicians - some played for fun, some for money. I had to engage and pay engineers to record my music in rented studio space.

A good friend set up a domain for me, a website to serve as a platform (if that's the word). I had to build and maintain a database of addresses of friends and fans who have said that they want to receive these emails. I had to write the verbiage, i.e, a weekly 'column' to elucidate the music, an on-going task at which I joyfully tinker almost every day. I conceive these emails about five or six weeks in advance, and each one is revised at least thirty times before I send it out. I'm not complaining. Believe it or not, revising is engrossing and always feels fun to me.

I now see that the sending of these weekly emails in this time of crisis is largely why I was composing for all those years. The goal was to offer a little 'joy in the morning.'

I set these words to music long ago, in 1975, as a deliberate gesture of reaction and rebellion against the avant garde style of writing that had been pressed upon me during my 'School of Music' years. It is very traditional, very conservative, with a straightforward melody, and a familiar chord progression. I was affirming my intention that my music would not be written in a bizarrely new, unique style never heard before, but rather as one small extension of an existing tradition.

To hear Heidi Miller and Chris Miller (no relation) singing, with an accompaniment performed by Beth Troendly, my setting of that verse (be patient, please; the music begins at :09).

Visit   http://www.sowash.com/recordings/mp3/joy.morning.mp3

To see a PDF of the score, visit http://www.sowash.-com/recordings/mp3/joy.morning.pdf

I'd love to know what you think about this music; feel free to contact me if you're inclined.

Anyone can be on my little list of recipients for these mpFrees (as I call these musical emails). To sign up, people can email me at rick@sowash.com, sending just one word: "Yes." I'll know what it means.

It's my policy nowadays to give away my life's work to anyone who is interested in discovering it. All my ideas came to me for free; I never paid a dime for any of them. In light of that, it seems to me that the right thing to do is to pass them along in turn for free.

This policy has brought many new friends into my life, people whom I would not have known otherwise. To my surprise, some of them insist on sending me money for my sheet music. I am not so lofty as to refuse to cash a check. I consider such contributions to be gifts flowing in my direction, just as my life's work makes gifts flowing out toward others from me.

Author Bio:

Rick Sowash is a composer/writer. He gives away his music and writings to anyone interested. He has composed 400+ musical works, 18 CDs and 7 books. Rick lives in Cincinnati with Jo, his wife who married in 1972.

http://www.sowash.com/

23

SET YOUR INNER SONGS FREE

Rebekah Maxner
Canada

The first time my father spent one-on-one time with me, I was thirteen years old and had just won a composition contest. He took me shopping in Halifax for a pair of shoes for the concert.

Sometimes, I've wondered over the years why I'm compelled to make music. Did my dad's attention galvanize my drive? Did I keep on making music to get more attention? From him and others? But I don't think so. I think my attachment to the piano had been formed a decade before that, before I can remember.

Our house was full of music. Two siblings, Phil and Judy, were taking piano lessons from a local professor of music and some of my earliest memories are of hearing them practicing. I started improvising on my own, pretending to play simply by imitating piano works and styles I'd heard. I'd created my own way of improvising. The music that came out of my fingers was gentle, expressive, and sometimes stormy. I was still a preschooler when Phil and Judy entered Acadia University's School of Music. I routinely heard music like Haydn's trumpet concerto and Chopin's Nocturnes.

Other siblings were into recorded music. They collected records from Queen to Pink Floyd to Elton John, from disco to gospel. I heard the best popular music and listened like a sponge. Music was also pivotal at my church. It was inspiring to be part of such heartfelt, spontaneous music making. All these early experiences drenched me with various traditions of music and spiraled into the sonic smorgasbord that eventually formed the basis of my musical imagination.

I believe that when music is part of a child's formative years, it becomes like a mother tongue. Music entered my heart like a language, and I can no more stop composing now than I can go mute. And the more time that passes, the more I realize that all the music I heard in my preschool years has had an impact on me and the styles I now compose.

For instance, I've wondered where my flair for jazz, blues, and popular styles comes from. Looking back, in my earliest years I was exposed to Black music on a familial level, through Nova Scotia's White family. With the recent Black Lives Matter movement, I had to take a long, hard look at the idea of cultural appropriation with jazz and blues. I've had to ask why I write in these styles? I think one reason is because from my earliest years, popular styles that emerged within Black culture were simply part of my everyday experience. I haven't yet finished thinking about these questions.

Piano lessons started when I was about six and Judy asked me whether I'd like to be her student. For about ten years she was my teacher. Eventually, I wasn't just improvising, I was composing. Phil was completing his Bachelor of Music degree in Composition at the University of Toronto. He'd come home for holidays and listen to my latest pieces. I remember playing my little piece, Waltz de Noel, and Phil pointed out that I was composing with I and V7 chords, but marveled that I'd never been taught about tonic and dominant, I was just making up music that sounded good by ear and by instinct.

At the age of twelve, several things happened: Judy showed me the movie *Amadeus* and I became obsessed with Mozart's music and the idea that I could become a real composer, and my school music teacher, Mrs. Pike, gave me an entry form for the Nova Scotia Music Educators' Association's Young Composer's Contest. I entered Dance for Piano and learned early in Grade 8 that I'd tied for first place. It was at this point in my life music became my primary focus.

My experience with university composition in the early 90s focused on applying compositional devices, like writing a tone row into an atonal composition, or creating serial music. I felt pressured to compose what I considered to be cerebral, brain, math music, like calculating a mind game on paper that may or may not have connected with an audience. After four years of frying my brain on music that just wasn't me, I gave up on composing and upon graduating, started teaching piano lessons in my own piano studio.

In my early years of teaching piano, I rarely felt like composing. It's like my heart was broken. If that's what composition was, I didn't want it. Instead, I turned my creativity to developing teaching aids to help my students understand music concepts. But little by little, I began to dabble in composing again.

The catalyst that finally hooked me was a children's book we got for our son, Patricia Godwin's *I Feel Orange Today*. I started creating piano pieces based on the poems, which were all about colours. But I was still insecure about what style I should compose. I believed that the only kind of music people would accept from a living composer was experimental, so my first attempts leaned that way. But then I began improvising a blues version, and this little blues piece changed the course of my professional composing career. *Blue Train* was published and noticed by Martha Hill Duncan, and she invited me to join *Red Leaf Pianoworks*.

For me, composition springs out of joy. I want to keep the playfulness and joy in my practicing, composing, and teaching, and pass this joy on like a legacy to my students and anyone who comes in contact with me musically through my *Piano at Play* blog, my compositions or on social media.

I believe music is for everyone, and everyone can experience the journey in their own way. I'd encourage you to sit at the piano, set yourself free of all expectations, and play. Just embrace the sounds that emerge from your fingers. At first it might sound a little messy, like you're about to take a picture with your camera but the image is blurry and out of focus. But if you trust the process, gradually your sounds will come more and more into focus, your music will gain clarity, gain confidence, and you will experience what it's like to create your own music at the piano. The key is to be curious and to trust that inside yourself you have a unique musical voice that has value and interesting things to say. The reason why we compose is because that voice wants to be heard. And we can make the world a better place when we set our inner songs free.

Author Bio:

Rebekah Maxner is a Nova Scotian piano teacher, blogger, and composer. Her jazzy and expressive piano music is listed and published by several conservatories and is heard in exams, festivals and recitals around the world.

https://rebekah.maxner.ca/intro/

24

BREAKING THROUGH THE WORLD OF
MUSIC CHAMPIONSHIP

Edy Rapika Panjaitan
Indonesia

An Indonesian pianist composes an anthem for OISAA. To what extent will music remain a heritage or a legacy to yourself, your loved ones, people around you, or even for the greater community? For which reasons were the major historical composers able to compose their masterpieces? Compose a sonata, prelude and fugue, or a symphony? These classical composers have inspired billions of people around the world and across generations. This is ultimately beneficial for the world's classical music heritage. I strongly believe those composers aimed for such legacy, or perhaps there is an untold story behind the masterpieces, and for music researchers, this provides such a wealth of information.

A year ago, in December 2020, I discovered a competition. It was a composition competition requiring participants to compose a March for overseas Indonesian students, known more famously as OISAA (Overseas Indonesian Students' Association Alliance), one of the largest Indonesian student communities. The committee opened selection for all Indone-sian students overseas. This competition inspired and moti-vated me as it was a great opportunity to meet the adjudication panel, all of whom were distinguished artists in Indonesia. At this stage, I was extremely motivated to compose my own legacy and write a masterpiece. The composition, a march, is aimed to be sung in every official meeting, after our own National Anthem, *Indonesia Raya*. With only a week remaining before the submission date, I put my internal struggles aside and pushed through.

At this time, I also researched the vision and mission of OISAA. As an overseas student, what was my role as a member of this body? Were the contributions that I had already given without knowing so? Perhaps my record of overseas study would help, and these questions helped me come up with my own power of 'Why'. I confidently believed my personal journey and the story behind my successful study as a music student abroad in China would surely help me along my future journey.

I would like to share my compositional process here. During the small hours of the morning, I began to pray and surrender my hopes that my song would be a blessing and inspirational to everyone who heard it. Fueled by passion, I began to jot down the lyrics. I tried to fit some words to musical phrases in the verse, and I finally found a musical voice. It reminded me of how Beethoven composed his own revolu-tionary musical motifs in his 5th Symphony – he is such an inspiration to me. After I finished the first stanza, I continued to the chorus the following day. I recall it as a particularly gloomy day, and I struggled with other aspects of study at the same time.

My professor pushed me to learn new piano pieces within a near-impossible five-day deadline, asking me to memorize them, in time to perform them for my final recital. I was incredibly frustrated at this time, though I always had support and encouragement from friends and teachers around me. When the pandemic kicked in, someone said, "Edy, you must strive for your recital. This is the best time to finish and don't procrastinate any further". I really did feel like giving it all up. But I persevered and practiced all day long, making myself sick in the process of doing so. But I kept on pushing forward.

All of a sudden, powerful lyrics came to mind complete with melody and rhythm. At this time, I was not sitting at the piano, but the inspiration came, and I wrote them down and recorded them on my phone. The very next day, I tried to write the chorus, and I began doing so at midnight. I figured this was the most tranquil time to compose. I tried to rouse up happiness and a grateful heart, fully giving love and joy to my music. I realize anything is possible, with conviction, dedication, perseverance, and passion.

This compositional format of a march is one of my personal favorites, and I kept thinking about the character of the march because so many composers have written marches. I wanted to be original, and thus channeled the sounds from my imagination. Every bar was rewritten and revised, changing rhythm, phrasing, articulation, and completely dismantling the melody and lyrics. I was required to create an accompaniment and did so at the piano, but I needed to compose a full score for orchestra using a midi-keyboard due to the looming deadline, but I promised myself I would continue to write an orchestral version in the future.

Marches are typically filled with energy and full of power. I put some accents in the percussion and imagined how I had once watched a carnival with marching band, so I scored for a brass section together with strings. The accompaniment is the main thing that instills this feeling, and the fact it will be sung by hundreds of thousands of students. However, it is necessary to help them with this rhythmic drive.

Within this strenuous week, I was able to finalize everything. I sent it to peers to get feedback before submitting. People said very favorable things to me and so I submitted it on the last day. Finally, the announcement came, and the ten finalists were announced – and behold, my name was amongst their number. The next round of the competition listed me as one of the five finalists – I was overjoyed. Eventually, the committee finally announced who the winner was. I waited with bated breath to discover that I was the winner of the competition - the anthem I composed for OISAA. It was one of the happiest occasions of my life. People were generous with their praise and encouragement. The jury enjoyed the energy of the piece, describing it as having a powerful simplicity.

I bow down and am thankful to God who gifted me a wonderful talent that I could never have dreamt of. Without the support from my teachers, family, and friends I could not have done this. So, my parting words are this: whatever your work is, from wherever you are, when you dedicate yourself and do this with love, everyone has the potential to leave a legacy to those who listen, perform, or those who appreciate your work. Keep making music; keep inspiring; and compose your own legacy.

Author Bio:

Edy Rapika Panjaitan is a Pianist, arranger, award winning composer, music educator, lecturer, international best-selling-author, Founder & CEO of Panda Piano Course

pandapianocourse.com

25

FROM SHE'S A SQUARE TO NO MORE PIZZA

Glory St. Germain
Canada

He wanted to be Elvis. He sang like Elvis, moved like Elvis, looked like Elvis, and he became known as Winnipeg's Elvis. As a singer/songwriter, this man had it all. And he had me...falling in love with his voice in the hit song he wrote called *She's a Square*. A rockabilly radio hit chart-topper that had me dancing like a crazy teenager, and which I still love listening to and dancing to today.

As a young musician and piano teacher, myself, I was always interested in learning the Why behind the story of song-writing, composing, and the strategies of putting together a melody, harmony, rhythmic elements, and creating this magical and memorable music that lives on forever. The music that moves you, makes you feel an emotion, reminds you of places you have been, things you've done, and people who you were with - creating memories at that moment in time.

Little did I know that *She's a Square* would impact my life at a deeper level than just the meaning of the words. The term 'square' originated with the American jazz community in the 1940s, referring to people out of touch or old-fashioned with musical trends.

Many years later, I had the opportunity to meet My Elvis as he was performing on stage, and I was modeling in the Miss Manitoba Pageant fashion show (and yes, my talent was playing piano). He was the singing host, and once again his voice captured my attention. In fact, so much so...that he invited me, 'the square girl' out for pizza. This musical genius was asking me out on a date to go for pizza.

And a short while later...I married the guy - the Legendary Ray 'Elvis' St. Germain.

Through the years, we traveled to many countries as I watched Ray perform on stage with countless standing ovations, hosting award-winning television shows, and recording his original music in the studio.

Yes, I'm proud of him. And I'm also grateful for the lessons he taught me.

As a musician, I witnessed the process of composing and song-writing from a different perspective, not just as an admirer of his music but how the music evolved. As Ray was booked into the recording studio to do a Christmas album, he sat down at the piano as he had to write three original songs in addition to the traditional favorites he was recording. The problem was, it was July - no snow, no holiday spirit, no feeling of festivities, so how could I help? First, I decided to make 'Christmas Dinner' in July, with all the trimmings and even decorations to help Ray get in the mood. Next, Ray invited me to be his writing partner on three Christmas songs which were going to be recorded the following week.

And so it happened, the collaboration between 'Ray and Glory' creating the music and words to three original songs: *I Lost One Reindeer, Christmas' Of Long Ago*, and *I'm Missing You This Christmas*. What an honor to write with the legendary Ray, whose song *She's a Square* had inspired me so long ago.

But wait...there's more. Not only did I get to write music with my husband, but our children David and Sherry produced the album and all five of our children and two grandchildren sang on the album too.

Composing is a creative process that is a gift from the universe. It comes through us as we experience the joy of sharing our music. As a music teacher and author of over fifty music theory books, composing played a huge part in the creation of the *Ultimate Music Theory Workbooks* Program.

I wanted to not only teach music theory but have students play compositions that showed the music theory concepts in music that were at their level to easily sight-read. Original compositions that allowed for analysis questions in showcasing music theory concepts in a step-by-step system that made sense to students of all learning styles and abilities.

Throughout the *Ultimate Music Theory Workbooks*, students can easily understand how music theory concepts are mapped out to help musicians structure a piece of music. In addition to understanding music theory concepts, how to compose or begin melody writing is another important aspect of teaching music theory. Throughout *the Ultimate Music Theory Supplemental Workbooks Series* (co-authored with Shelagh McKibbon-U'Ren), we developed an easy program called *ICE: Imagine, Compose, Explore* that takes students from the *Music Theory*

Beginner ABC Series through Prep, Levels 1 - 8, and the all-in-one *Complete Supplemental Workbook.*

Why teach music theory and composition? Because you never know what inspiration and foundation you are creating for your students as a music educator. Many of my students have become composers, including Connor Derraugh whose story you read earlier in this book. Sometimes you compose because of a feeling that moves you beyond words and music is the only escape. Sometimes you compose music to teach a concept or to share your heritage.

My husband Ray, Canadian Country Music Hall of Fame Inductee, has received numerous awards for his compositions, including the Aboriginal Order of Canada for his original song *The Metis* which tells the story of his heritage. What legacy do I leave behind? My work in composing a music program to support future generations of composers and the memory of one special piece of music. You may be thinking *She's a Square* but in fact, although that did get me started on my path to composing, a memorable simple piece I wrote in my very first *Ultimate Music Theory Basic Rudiments Workbook* was called *No More Pizza.* Why?

Because just as I supported my husband through all his years of writing, performing, and touring, he too supported me in all my years of writing, teaching, and composing pieces for my workbooks. His way of supporting me was simply to have dinner ready so I could continue to write. Just as I finished writing a short piece in C minor for an analysis question in the Basic Workbook, my husband proudly announced that dinner had arrived "PIZZA'S HERE" (yes, that's his way of cooking dinner - ordering delivery). So, without further ado, I named my piece *No More Pizza* (as it had been the dinner option for a week), and gratefully sat down with my husband to yet another delightful pizza dinner together.

Why teach composing? It is a way to embrace musicianship at a deeper level. To learn more about how you can teach melody writing, visit UltimateMusicTheory.com. Teach with Passion.

Author Bio:

Glory St. Germain ARCT RMT MYCC UMTC, International Bestselling Author, fifty plus Ultimate Music Theory Books, *The Power of Why Musicians Series*, and Host of Global Music Summits. Glory is the creator of the UMT Certification Course, UMTC Elite Educator Program, and UMT Teachers Membership and is an Expert Music Business Coach.

https://UltimateMusicTheory.com/

AFTERWORD: THE MAGIC OF COMPOSERS

Glory St. Germain

Have you ever felt like your voice, emotions, or ideas should be heard? Not just in your head but expressed through music? Me too.

Composing can feel lonely at times, with so many ideas and no one to talk to who truly understands the process. You may feel isolated with no one to give you a 'high five' to celebrate your wins. It's not always an easy place to be. But through desire, dedication, and determination...you too can become a composer.

Are you ready to jump into composing and go for the ultimate musical ride of your life?

Fasten your seat belt because you are about to experience every emotion you can ever imagine. It is exhilarating, scary, rewarding, discouraging, empowering, profitable, and every conceivable array of emotions imaginable. And it is totally worth it.

By creating your musical legacy, you can help others feel empowered, become confident, build knowledge, and provide them with an opportunity to be a part of something bigger, a movement of enriching lives through music composition.

Through my musical journey, life taught me five techniques to L-E-A-R-N

L – Listen to your inner voice when you hear that cry for help. "Why should I become a composer/songwriter and express my ideas, my emotions, my story?"

What happens when people don't engage or listen to the music you are writing? How do you cope with failure?

What's your mindset? A fixed mindset believes that abilities are fixed, and your goal is to prove yourself. A growth mindset understands your abilities can be developed through effort and education. Your Mindset - Affects the Way You Lead Your Life.

Change the *I can't* attitude to the *I can* attitude. Your skills can be developed through your direct success path to becoming the best musician, composer, or teacher that you can be.

Will your composition be a masterpiece? No, not yet, but with a growth mindset, when you are open to learning and listening, you will succeed.

E – Educate yourself using ICE – Imagine, Compose & Explore. All compositions begin with an idea, no matter how small, from a simple four note motif to a title of a story you want to tell. Compose Things Differently and Compose Different Things.

Imagine - Your idea may start with a song title, lyrics, a melody waiting for a foundation of harmonic variations, or a chord structure begging for a melodic line above it.

Compose - You may play/sing your composition and record it. Write it down on paper or compose directly on a computer program - discover what works best for you.

Explore - You may discover new ways of expressing your music, collaborating with others, and stretching outside your comfort zone. Share your music with the world.

A – Articulate clearly the meaning and message of the

composition. The single most important skill every composer needs is the ability to articulate in a clear and concise language so the listener will fully appreciate the music.

Articulation refers to different effects on how the music communicates to the listener. That articulation will elicit a mood or create an experience for the listener that may be completely different from what the composer may have wished to communicate.

How effective is your articulation in communicating with your listeners?

Analyze your composition. Are you composing just for yourself or to share your message, feelings, or ideas with the world? We need to be open to interpretations. The truth is the most important thing to analyze is the impact your music has on you first, and then on the listeners of your music. Why are you composing?

R – Relate your composition to the elements of music that serve you best in expressing your idea - your message - your story.

Why do we have to relate music to the composition process? There is no end to creativity. Can you imagine if there was?

Ah, Boring...Who's with me?

One magic word that you can implement into your composing process is storytelling.

Storytelling is a powerful technique, a means to communicate ideas so you can relate information in a memorable way. Storytelling allows you to engage emotionally and experience the music in a powerful and personal way.

Storytelling is learning, creating, and expressing your own story. As listeners relate to your music, they will hear the message, feel the emotion, groove to the tune, dance up a storm, hold it in their heart dearly...as you had intended for them to relate to the music.

N – NEPD Never-Ending Professional Development. In the

empowering words of philosopher Jim Rohn, "It's not what you get, it's what you become."

How can you become more than you are, a better musician, composer, educator? How can you serve others by helping them set goals and learn through gratitude? Goal Setting alone is not enough.

"Goal Setting with Accountability and Direction is the Greatest Motivation for Achievement" ~ Glory St. Germain

The fact that you are here, reading this book, shows that you are committed to continuing your education. This speaks volumes about you, your growth mindset, and your dedication to continue learning and serving others through your music.

I'm on a mission to accelerate your growth, to remove the headaches and confusion of creating your own musical legacy all by yourself. *The Power of Why Musicians Book Series* is compiled to give you the exact process techniques that others have followed that turned their goals to gratitude in achieving successful and profitable businesses.

Now is the time to implement the lessons you have learned and help others by giving them an opportunity to learn from your expertise, your music, and your success.

Become A Master Musician and Compose with Passion.

Why implement and L-E-A-R-N the greatest lessons ever? So, you can:

• Listen to your heart. Take your composition process from confused to confident.

• Educate yourself. Use the ICE method to move from frustrated to fantastic.

• Articulate clearly. Change your mindset from scared to successful.

• Relate to listeners. Connect to change lives from overwhelm to opportunity.

• NEPD. Compose your music with passion to shift from goals to gratitude.

ACKNOWLEDGMENTS

Acknowledgements

I want to thank all the musicians for being willing to share their ideas, their expertise, and ultimately, their stories of inspiration, and most importantly their, WHY.

Their WHY became the strategies that led them to their success. I am grateful to them and proud to share the 'power of why' their goals became the reality in this book.

I want to thank my UMT Dream Team Shelagh McKibbon-U'Ren, Joanne Barker, Migelie Luna, and Julie-Kristin Hardt who helped me to implement these ideas and share them with the world.

Thank you to the hundreds of musicians, entrepreneurs, teachers, and students that I have learned from through the years who gave me the framework to build my company, write the *Ultimate Music Theory Program*, UMT Courses, UMT Membership, and compile the *Power of Why Musicians Book Series*.

Thank you to our editors Wendy H. Jones and Lisa McGrath for their guidance, expertise, and countless hours in making this book possible.

It is with gratitude to everyone who has taken the risk to dream big and follow their heart to become a musician, composer, educator, or entrepreneur, and generously leave their legacy by enriching lives through music education.

ABOUT THE AUTHOR

About the Author

Glory St. Germain ARCT RMT MYCC UMTC is the Founder/Author of 50+ Books of the *Ultimate Music Theory Program* and Founder of the *Magic of Music Movement*. She is on a mission to help 1 million teachers create a legacy through their business. She is the host of the *Global Music Teachers Summits, Course Creator, Expert Music Teachers Coach,* Publisher of the *Ultimate Music Theory Series,* and an International Best-selling Author in *The Power of Why Musicians Series*, an anthology of global authors/musicians sharing their stories of inspiration.

She is the founder of the UMTC ELITE EDUCATOR PROGRAM - A Business Accelerator in knowledge and expert strategies for teachers to use in order to run their successful music studios. She empowers educators to elevate their income, impact their teaching, and build their expert music business while enjoying personal time for self-care, family, and pursuing
other passions.

In addition, Glory is an NLP Practitioner (Neuro-Linguistic Programming) and has taught piano, theory, and music for young children for over twenty years and contributed as a composer. She has served in various leadership positions to support music education organizations.

Glory has spoken on many international stages presenting workshops and is passionate about enriching lives through music education.

Glory loves learning and especially loves books on business and psychology. Mindset is a subject she believes has the potential to change our outcomes. Mindset is limited only by our own thinking. She is a positive mental attitude advocate and strongly believes that we need to see mindset as a priority, not only for ourselves but also for how we help others think, learn, and grow.

She is married to Ray St. Germain, a professional multi-award-winning entertainer and Canadian Country Music Hall of Fame inductee. They have five musically talented children, many grandchildren, and the family continues to grow.

Glory lives her life with gratitude, passion, and serving others through her work.

https://UltimateMusicTheory.com

ALSO BY GLORY ST. GERMAIN

The Power of Why: Why 21 Musicians Created a Program

The Power of Why: Why 23 Musicians Crafted a Course

Made in the USA
Las Vegas, NV
18 August 2021